MW01006594

GET HIGH NOW

GET HIGH NOW

James Nestor

CHRONICLE BOOKS

SAN FRANCISCO

Not all of the exercises and activities in this book are suitable for everyone. Your physical condition and health are important factors in determining which, if any, may be appropriate for you. This or any exercise and activity program may result in injury. The author and publisher of this book disclaim any liability from any injury that may result from the use, proper or improper, of any exercise or activity contained in this book. The accuracy and completeness of the information provided and the opinions stated herein are not guaranteed or warranted to produce any particular results, and the advice and strategies contained herein may not be suitable for every individual. Please consult your professional health care provider for information and advice on the suitability of any exercise or activity program.

Library of Congress Cataloging-in-Publication Data

Nestor, James.
    Get high now without drugs : featuring more than 200 sensory tips and tricks for visual stimulation, lucid dreaming, compressing time, meditation, and more / by James Nestor.
        p. cm.
ISBN 978-0-8118-6713-9
1. Altered states of consciousness. I. Title.

BF1045.A48N47 2009
154.4--dc22
2009024550

Designed by Suzanne LaGasa
Typeset by Janis Reed
This book was typeset in Poynter, Interstate and Springfield.

Manufactured in China

10 9 8 7 6 5

Chronicle Books LLC
680 Second Street
San Francisco, CA 94107
www.chroniclebooks.com

TABLE OF CONTENTS

213 CALMING HIGHS

INTRODUCTION

Research for this book began two million years ago. There, on a swampy marshland of Tanzania, a monobrowed *homo habilis* rested his stumpy torso against a rock outcropping and gazed on the weedy pools of black water that surrounded him. Something was happening to his brain. Something fantastic. Was it caused by the quick breaths he took from his wide-nostriled nose? The fistfuls of ants he had gobbled earlier in the day? The natural radon gas emitting from the granite beneath his feet? He knew not, but he liked it—he liked the surge of endorphins in his blood, the quickened pulse of his heart against his hairy chest, the levitational light-headedness in his fist-size brain. He felt good. He was *high*.

And so was I, two million years later, crouched over a wall-size file cabinet in the dusty corner office of an abandoned house in the Hollywood Hills. I was spending my summer cleaning out an estate house my family had just inherited. My uncle had lived there, an eccentric playboy of the old school whose appetite for seducing local starlets was second only to his unending thirst for amassing antiques. And books. *Thousands* of them. Lining the shelves, stuffed into closets, scattered in the halls, on subjects ranging from Ming porcelain to ancient marine navigation, Confederate guns to Oceanic mythology.

There were also books on meditation. Books and cassettes, record albums, files, and mounds of college-ruled notepads filled with handwritten instructions for things like Transcendental Meditation, yoga poses, extrasensory perception, relaxation, meditations for sex, for stress, getting rich. One pamphlet caught my attention—it described a breathing technique. Its aged, yellow corners cracked as I opened the pages. The exercise seemed simple. So I crossed my legs, arched my back, and began.

Deep breaths, very deep breaths: ten slow, fifteen fast, and back again. Repeat. I closed my eyes. I felt dizzy, a bit lightheaded, but I kept going. Sometime later I felt I had left the room and gone somewhere else: a place of different colors, different sounds, different feelings. A *better* place.

When I opened my eyes my body tingled, the room was brighter. I had trouble standing up while I walked to the porch. Once there I looked below me: The Los Angeles skyline, which earlier had appeared so muddled and post-apocalyptic, took on an ethereal glow, like it was lit from within. Something had happened to my brain. Something fantastic. "Shit," I thought, "I am *high*." And all just by breathing.

• ✳ •

I took my uncle's notes, books, and records back home to San Francisco. After a few days I felt less like I was perusing 1970s meditation techniques and more like I was skimming an abridged encyclopedia of human history. From Africa to Chile, China to Papua New Guinea, the notes illustrated how altering consciousness was not just a recreational hobby for a few wide-eyed mystics, but a central goal for every society since pre-history. As such, over the last ten thousand years cultures around the world had developed meditations, dances, postures, breathing techniques—each designed specifically to induce trance, stimulate the brain and body, and evoke an ecstatic experience. To get us *high*.

My uncle—like me—never had an interest in drugs. Perhaps drugs seemed too easy, a predictable and trendy cop-out; perhaps he had seen too many friends in the 1960s destroyed by them. I don't know. As an antique collector and recreational anthropologist his interest was in the arcane, ancient ways of doing things. And since many of the most effective ways of inducing altered states of consciousness in the past were done without drugs, it was these highs he researched.

He began his work at a good time. In the 1960s and '70s, studying highs seemed a national obsession: Academics were exploring out-of-body experiences; scientists were locating the chemicals in the brain that induced ecstasy; even the military was in on it, spending millions of dollars exploring extrasensory perception. They were all trying to demystify the mystical experience, to finally peg some objective proof on what had before always been ineffable subjective experiences. They wanted to know if meditation, breathwork, chanting, and all these other ancient methods were just self-suggestive hallucinations, or if something else, something physical, was going on as well.

Their discoveries were shocking. EKGs, EEGs, and fMRIs taken of people practicing ancient highs showed a physiological transformation. In certain methods of breathwork, for instance, the pulse softened, blood flowed more quickly, the rhythm of the organs aligned, weird stuff—like cholesterol levels dropping—occurred, and areas of the brain that were seldom used began to light up. While getting high, people were going *somewhere else*, and their bodies seemed to be metamorphosing. And all just through inhaling and exhaling or looking or listening or *thinking* in a certain way—simple methods known for thousands of years but since forgotten in western society.

My uncle's notes ended around 1980. Whether he had finally found what he was looking for or had grown weary of the subject I'll never know, but I have a feeling it was the latter. By the early 1980s many of the top scientists who had studied highs in the past few decades had moved on to more conventional, grant-friendly pursuits. By the early 1990s, the military pulled much of its funding from its ESP labs. Another group took over the study of altered states of consciousness: the New Age movement.

Centered around cosmology and esotericism, New Agers explored the same ancient "highs" as the scientists had in the 1960s and '70s, but did so subjectively, explaining the purpose, mental and physical effects of these techniques, and their results in decidedly unscientific ways. Most New Age practitioners were suspicious of western medicine, instead opting for folk remedies, mysticism, and psychic intuition. As such, the study of altered states of consciousness (which came to be identified with the New Age movement) moved from a scientific inquiry *back* into an unquantifiable, indescribable subjective experience, where it had been for thousands of years throughout history. For better or for worse, by the 1980s and '90s getting high was re-mystified.

• ✳ •

A month after returning from Hollywood I was hosting a cocktail party at my house. I noticed a friend on the couch laughing uncontrollably. She was reading my uncle's notes, which I had inadvertently left out on the coffee table in a panic of pre-party cleaning. She started reading them aloud. Everyone listened. They, like me, found the highs fascinating, and yet totally ridiculous at the same time. Could you really go out-of-body from spinning around in a circle for twenty minutes? Does nutmeg make you hallucinate? Would drinking a schizophrenic's blood induce hour-long paranoid dream-visions? We laughed them off together. After the party I packed the notes into a box, plopped them in the garage, and moved on.

But I couldn't stop thinking about them. In particular, I couldn't explain what had happened to me during my impromptu breathing exercise on a dusty office floor in the Hollywood Hills. The feeling was of something odd, something other. It creeped me out—but it also made me curious. I began to wonder, as loony as so many of the highs sounded, if some of the other highs could really alter consciousness, change my physiology, make me "see" music and "hear" colors the way the ancients described. After all, most of the highs had been around thousands of years—were all those people in China, Africa, Europe, and South America crazy? Or were they on to something?

• ✳ •

The notes, books, and records in my uncle's library were merely a starting point; most highs in this book were culled from a variety of outside sources.

While a few of the more transformational highs necessitate months-long trips of soul-searching in deserts and jungles, most of them are simple, quick, and can take place almost anywhere: on the couch, sleeping, in your car, alone, at your office desk, in a boring quarterly meeting, during an interview, while reading this book, *any time*. All with the aim: *Get High Now* without drugs.

A few methods (giraffe marrow, bee stings, exposure to inescapable physical trauma) have been included simply because they seemed so shockingly wrong. I've called these out as such, and in some cases refrained from providing instructions because I do not want you to do them. Your mother doesn't want you to do them. The ER doesn't want you to do them. These highs are included because I thought they were fascinating, funny, or just jaw-droppingly disgusting. Consider them historical and/or anthropological oddities, like old surgical tools on display at a museum—things to be marveled at but never, ever actually used.

There are no controlled substances in this book. Including them would be counter to my uncle's research, my interests, and the general thrust of this project. These drugs are so obvious, too *easy*, and often destructive; worst of all, they are boring. There are a few entries (toads, kava, Russian reindeer urine) that, while legal, contain ingredients like dimethyltryptamine (DMT), kavalactones, and muscarine that could certainly be considered "drugs" that get you "high." But foods like coffee, herbal teas, and coriander also contain ingredients that get you "high." So how did I draw the line? Totally subjectively: Entries I found intriguing and/or unexpected I included in the same spirit as giraffe marrow, as subjects of wonder rather than practice.

A few of the more arcane entries, such as ants and salamander, can be spotty in their specifics not for lack of effort, but because there has been such little research done on them. Consider these highs frontier science, and you, little trippers, are the pioneers.

HighLab: Getting Results

Yeah yeah yeah, you're thinking, *but do any of these highs actually work?* At least that's what I wanted to know. To find out I created HighLab, a rotating circle of writers, teachers, designers, surfers, fools, and anyone else bored enough to come by my house on an occasional Sunday or Tuesday night to try out this stuff firsthand.

For two months HighLab experimented with audio brainwave stimulation, Indian breathing techniques, inversion, dream work, spices, insects, and some other methods which shall remain unmentioned (please, don't ask). At the very first session, we were confused and a bit frightened to discover that Binaural Beats (see page 48) actually seemed to produce a three-dimensional imagined tone that floated outside of the brain. By the second session we were on to *Kriya,* a form of breathwork that induced within every HighLab member a rush so completely disarming that hearing, vision, and feeling were suspended for moments at a time. (I recall after a twenty-minute session one member smiling and speaking with numb, lisping lips, "I than't fewl ma fu'ing face.") The dreams we all had that night were shimmering and lucid, otherworldly and beautiful. Yes, *really.*

I remember on the final session laying on my back on my living room floor, lights down, pink noise pulsing through the headphones, surrounded by other HighLab members in the same position, the same trance. In the final weeks, HighLab felt as though it had become less of a drug-free high-inducing experiment and more an anthropological dig, each of us unearthing the exact same ecstatic experiences felt by millions of people over thousands of years. On that Sunday night, laying there, I remember imagining that I was tracing back through our collective DNA, and, for a moment, was standing on a granite outcropping peering into the long, muddled eyes of our monobrowed *homo habilis* ancestors. The transcendent highs *homo habilis* had experienced, I, too, was sharing. A line was connected, a circle closed. I approached him and hugged his hairy body.

And then I sat up, took off the headphones, and opened my eyes. *What the f**?!?* Monobrowed ancestors? Collective DNA? Closed circles? What was all this nonsense? Was I losing my mind? I took a deep breath, came to my senses, and realized it was OK. I was fine. It wasn't my fault.

I was just gettin' *high*.

• ✳ •

A Word of Advice

"What you give is what you get."

The Jam, "Start!"

Most methods in this book will only be as effective as you wish them to be. Take a half-assed approach to doing them and you'll get half-assed results. Sun & Moon Breath, Qigong Diaphragmatic Breath, and other ancient breathing techniques may take just a few minutes. The more immersive, cathartic, and potentially life-changing techniques such as Diekman Contemplative Meditation and Compressed Time can take hours. All of the them require concentration.

So turn off your cell phone, pull up a chair, and tell your friends and family you'll be away for a bit. The world won't miss you, but you may miss some hidden wonders of the world if you don't *give in* a little, if you don't at least try to *go there* with us. You may only have everything to lose. *Start!*

KEY

- ◉ View at Gethighnow.com
- 🔊 Listen at Gethighnow.com
- 👥 Try it with a friend
- ☺ HighLab Favorite

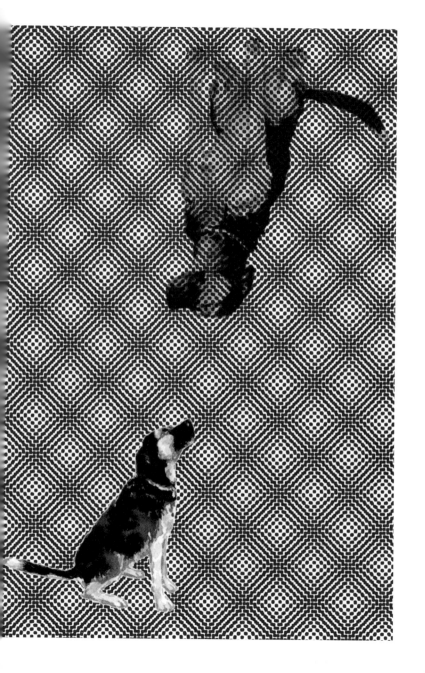

Chapter One:

SENSORY HIGHS

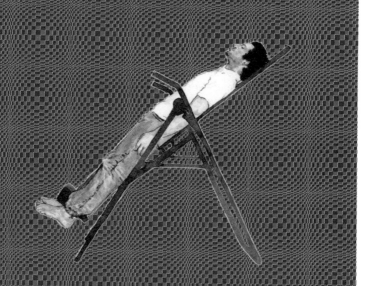

HYPNAGOGIC INDUCTION

A state of auditory, visual, and sometimes tactile reverie, hypnagogia occurs in the "no man's land" between wakefulness and sleep. It's there, in this semi-conscious state, that the mind runs amok, offering wild visions as well as occasional glimpses of lucidity into your thoughts, feelings, and life. For hundreds of years, artists, mathematicians, and scientists have looked to hypnagogia for inspiration. Artist Matthew Barney uses his hypnagogic visions as a muse to guide his layered, weirdly imaginative films. Einstein solved numerous mathematical problems in a hypnagogic state. But us, we just use it to get high.

Get High Now

Dr. Charles Tart, a psychologist who has experimented with altered states of consciousness throughout the 1960s to the present, developed a method to attune and prolong the hypnagogic state. It works like this: Before going to sleep at night, lie on your back on your bed. Raise one arm in the air, perpendicular to your body. Hold it comfortably, bending slightly at the elbow. Relax and let your mind drift. When your body begins to fall asleep, the muscles in your arm will release, causing the arm to fall and wake you up. By doing this you will allow your brain to enter a hypnagogic state without falling asleep. When you come-to, you will be able to remember what transpired in the hypnagogia, and with practice, will be able to control subject matter and process, leading to some very weird lucid trips.

> **Fun Fact:** *Thomas Edison (1847–1931), famed American inventor, used hypnagogia to think through a number of his 1,093 U.S.-patented inventions. At night he'd sit in a chair holding a glass bottle in one hand. He would then close his eyes and wallow in hypnagogia trying to work out solutions until he lost consciousness, which would cause his muscles to relax and the bottle to slip from his hand. This would wake him up. He'd review what transpired in his hypnagogia, then do it all again.*

PRISONER'S CINEMA

After extended periods in the darkness of solitary confinement, prisoners often experience phosphene hallucinations—psychedelic light patterns and colors produced by the eye's retinal cells. What's happening is the retinal ganglion cells (which transmit visual information from the eye to the brain) in the prisoners' eyes grow agitated with the lack of visual data. The cells are used to constantly processing visual information, and to keep themselves active they begin to send false "light" information to the brain. The result is an involuntary hallucination of flashing colored light patterns that plays continuously, whether eyelids are open or closed.

Prisoners aren't the only ones lucky enough to have front-row seats to the "cinema." Anyone can get a phosphene high, anytime and anywhere. Isaac New-

ton's favorite method, and the easiest way, is to apply soft pressure on the lids of your closed eyes. This exercise stimulates the ganglions to send phony light information to the brain—just like solitary confinement but with more controllable and potent results.

Get High Now

Go wash your hands. Sit in a chair and close your eyes. Take the tips of your fingers and *very lightly* massage the corners of your covered eyeballs. Do this for thirty seconds. Soon you will be engulfed in a dreamland of mandalas and paisleys and other mystical wonders.

If you are ever tripping in the office and a coworker inquires if you're OK, simply turn to him, continuing to rub the corners of your closed eyelids, and in a soft voice say, "It's cool. I'm just getting a phosphene high." He won't bother you again. Ever.

Bonus High

While showering, close your eyes and face the shower nozzle. The gentle force of water will beat down on your eyelids, creating a fantastic, full-color light show on par with the most decadent prog-rock concert.

> **Fun Fact**: *Ancient Greeks were big fans of phosphene hallucinations, and it is from the Greek words* phos *(light) and* phainein *(to show) that the phenomenon gets its name.*

ANTS

In May 2008 the Government of Dubai passed an ordinance prohibiting smoking among children thirteen or younger. This law did not prohibit the smoking of tobacco, but red ants. According to a government survey, ant smoking was at epidemic levels: 33 percent of all children in Dubai reported to have at least tried a puff. What ant smokers seek is formic acid, which ants store in their poison glands and release to kill prey. When burnt, formic acid releases fumes that induce a spacey, mildly euphoric high.

Native Americans in California ingested live ants to provoke altered states of consciousness. This is what anthropologist JP Harrington discovered in 1917 while researching the Kitanemuk Indians, a small tribe who lived in the Mojave Desert of southern California. As part of an initiation ceremony, young Kitanemuks would fast for three days. On the third morning of the fast, the youth would lie down and swallow live ants fed to them by elders. Once ingested, and still alive, the ants would begin to bite the stomach lining trying to get out. In this process lactones related to nepetalactone would be released. Nepetalactone is the same organic compound that gets both cats (and people) stoned off catnip (page 221). According to the Kitanemuk Indians, enough of nepetalactone-like lactones could lead fasting youths on psychedelic dream visions.

Ingesting live ants could also give spiritual power, or so thought the Tübatulabal Indians who lived alongside the Kitanemuks in the southern Sierra Nevada. There, youths would fast for three days and enter a sweat lodge. According to author Richard Rudley, a youth's grandfather would then feed the initiate "seven balls of eagle down, each containing five yellow ants." The youth would be shaken to provoke the ants into biting the stomach lining. The Tübatulabal believed doing this would give the youth spiritual power and allow him to enter into a night of rich dream visions. In the morning, the youth would vomit up the down and recap the previous night's experiences.

Get High Now

Dubai youth smoke red "Samsun" ants. The exact species of ants the Tübatulabal and Kitanemuks used is not known, though Richard Rudley suggests it is possibly the yellow honey ant. What this means: it's time to get researching. Tonight, leave some honey on your windowsill. Wait three days for ants to collect. Light up or start swallowing.

SUN & MOON BREATH

Tantrics are followers of the mystical Asian religious philosophy of *Tantra*. In Tantra the universe is controlled by the divine energy of Hindu gods Shakti, the celestial feminine spirit, and Shiva, "the supreme one." Tantra does not exist within but alongside major Eastern religions such as Hinduism and Buddhism, influencing each with its powerful yoga and meditation exercises.

Tantrics believe that breathing through different nostrils can stimulate—or relax—different energies in the body. Inhaling the Moon Breath through your left nostril, they posit, can help regulate your body's natural functions, increase intuition and creativity, and calm the nervous system. The Sun Breath, inhaled through the right nostril, stimulates the vasomotor system (which dilates and constricts the blood vessels) and fortifies the body with energy. As such, Moon Breath is suggested for calmer, more contemplative endeavors like reading and meditating; Sun Breath is a good preparation before participating in sports, eating, or making whoopee.

Get High Now

Using your right hand, place your thumb over your right nostril and inhale through your left nostril as you would a normal breath. Exhale at the same rate through the same nostril. Feel your body grow calmer, your mind more relaxed. After a few breaths, place your index finger over your left nostril and breath in and out through the right nostril in the same manner. Feel your body flush with energy. Breathing more quickly through the right nostril will give you more of a rush; breathing more slowly through the left nostril is calming. Play with it.

THETA WAVE
BRAIN SYNCHRONIZATION ⑨

The human brain produces different levels of electrical activity depending on the amount of information it is processing. During a detailed task, it lights up with electrical charges as it sends and receives messages at a high concentration, its neurons firing in quick succession. While in a relaxed state of sleep, it glows dimmer, its neurons firing less often. This brainwave activity is calculated by electroencephalographs (EEGs), machines that gather data from electrodes adhered to the skull and measure the frequency (the amount of electric activity per unit of time) in Hertz (for more about Hertz, see page 55). Measurements of electrical activity in the brain are more commonly referred to as *brainwaves.*

Throughout the day, the brain lingers between four different types of brainwave patterns: Beta, the normal, awake consciousness associated with busy tasks; Alpha, the relaxed and reflective state, like those induced by closing the eyes during waking hours; Theta, a deeply relaxed state associated with meditation and some sleep states; and Delta, deep, dreamless sleep. The higher the Hertz, the more concentrated the brain activity. Beta waves usually hover around 12 to 30 Hz while Delta waves lull around 3 Hz and below.

Theta waves (at around 4 to 7 Hz) are the sweet spot for many brain functions. There we often experience extreme relaxation, creativity, as well as vibrant mental imagery.

For the past forty years or so scientists have experimented with different audio techniques to induce Theta waves. One technique is to play a specific audio rhythm to replicate the 4 to 8 Hz frequency of the Theta brainwaves. By doing so, scientists hoped to lull the brain into the Theta state on command. Fantastically, it works.

Get High Now

The track at Gethighnow.com is a replication of a Theta wave entrainment rhythm first created by scientists to lull patients into a deep, colorful, creative state. It's basic, *real* basic, but it works. Sit somewhere comfortable and listen to it for ten minutes. Concentrate on the moment. Feel your brain hemispheres merging, neurons firing, synapses synapting, and body slowly, slowly drifting, drifting, further, further . . .

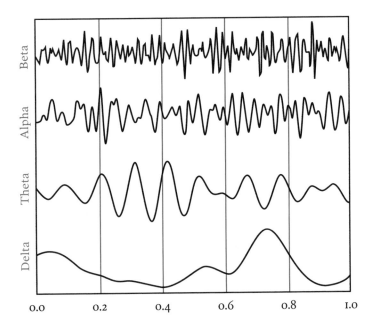

CASTANEDIAN SELF-PROGRAM DREAM CONTROL

In the 1970s, the books of Carlos Castaneda spawned a million New Age "Don Juanabees," people who left their comfy suburban homes for the deserts of the Southwest to follow the teachings of Castaneda and his mystical Yaqui Indian sage, Don Juan. Most Don Juanabees burned out by the 1980s but some stayed in Sedona, Santa Fe, and Taos, where today they sell hand-woven friendship bracelets at flea markets, practice gemstone therapy in strip malls, and live in messy communal apartments by the airport.

But enough about them. Let's talk about Carlos. Along with munching peyote on days-long vision quests, Castaneda was also an active lucid dreamer. He even wrote a book about it, *The Art of Dreaming*, which, like most of his writing, is so filled with conceited self-analysis, clichéd analogies, and misplaced conjunctive adverbs it is almost entirely unreadable. Luckily you don't have to. We've distilled a few lessons below.

Get High Now

Put a pen and pad of paper by your bed. Before sleeping, pick a subject on which to concentrate. Let's say, carrots. As you get tired, think about carrots. When you fade into sleep, hold on tighter to an image of carrots, to eating carrots, boiling carrots. Carrots. Tell yourself the first thing you will think about in the morning will be carrots. As you first enter a dream, immediately try to find carrots. Look around. Stay focused. When you awake either in the morning or during the course of sleep at night, write down every detail you remember of your dreams. Chances are, you will have dreamt of carrots. Continue this process the next night and night after that. Keep trying to dream of carrots. As the week progresses, switch subjects. With practice you will be able to dream about carrots or anything else you want, work out problems that have been nagging you, or just have fun.

MIRACLE FRUIT
(Sideroxylon dulcificum)

This West African berry has been celebrated since the 1700s for its "miraculous" ability to transform the bitterest foods into the sweetest of delights. How it works is not entirely known. Some scientists believe the miraculin protein in the berry temporarily alters the structure of our taste buds, making sour and bitter foods taste sweet. Göran Hellekant, a professor of physiology and pharmacology at the University of Minnesota, argues that miraculin may be activating the "sweet receptor membrane," which sits on the taste buds of our tongues and is usually only stimulated by genuinely sweet food. Hellekant argues that miraculin may distort these receptors to recognize bitter foods as sweet.

Distorting receptors? Sounds dangerous, eh? Worry not: Miracle fruit is totally safe, so says Linda Bartoshuk at the University of Florida's Center for Smell and Taste, who has extensively studied the berry. Sweet!

Get High Now

Processed miracle fruit tablets are available at select health food stores and online. HighLab prefers eating the berries fresh. A number of orchards offer overnight delivery of berries implicitly for "taste-tripping" parties.

HighLab attended one of these parties in August 2008 and found miracle fruit lived up to much of its hype: brie cheese tasted like sweet chocolate; wine was transformed into grape juice; cheap tequila became full-bodied, syrupy, and delicious. While other foods proved less edible (vinegar, *yuck!*), most foods we tried were transformed in flavor in one way or another.

Fresh miracle fruit berries cost around $3 each when ordered online. Gather a group of friends and host your own taste-tripping party—it will be a night you and your taste buds will never forget.

> **Fun Fact**: *During the 1970s, health-food companies attempted to use miracle fruit as a low-calorie sugar alternative. Just as the use of miracle fruit proved plausible, research was stopped and production ceased. Some blame the demise on interference by the sugar industry, who was nervous miracle fruit would bite into profits. The Federal Drug Administration has still yet to release any files on the subject.*

WINDOW ROUGHING ♫

You're driving in your car. The windows are rolled down a bit. You speed up. Suddenly an intense *thwomping* rattles your ears and shakes your head. You start to get *high*; you start Window Roughing.

Almost everyone who drives has experienced at least a minor Window Rough. What's happening is the air within the cabin is leaving quicker than the outside air is coming in. This creates a vacuum, signaled by an intense *thwomping* in the cabin of the car. Upon entering the rough most people cancel this vacuum by simply raising or lowering the window a few inches. Those people are quitters and fools. Clever folks (you) know that by continuing the rough, the vacuum will eventually begin to affect the body's endolymph—the fluid in our ears that helps us monitor balance. This will cause initial bouts of dizziness, disorientation, and nausea. Extended endolymph disruption via roughing in some cases can lead to minor audio and visual hallucinations.

Get High Now

Cars rough in varying degrees. Some might rough extremely well while others don't rough at all. The most important factor in roughing is window position, which can vary greatly depending on the model of the car. Try first to keep all windows rolled up and adjust just the driver's side. If that doesn't work, try other windows. Speed and wind velocity will also affect the duration and quality of the *rough*.

HighLab: Getting Results

HighLab attempted roughing in 17 different cars of various makes, models, and years. We found the car most conducive to the practice was a 2003 Volkswagen Golf TDI running on biodiesel. (The biodiesel likely only affecting the experiment by earning us eco-points.) When driven on the freeway at a speed of 53 mph with the driver's-side window rolled down about 25 percent, the entire cabin began *thwomping* with great intensity—inducing such dizziness and disorientation for the driver that he had to pull over at Trader Joe's and buy some off-label Danish beer and raw almonds before continuing. Other cars that roughed exceptionally well were a 1977 Mercedes 300D (driver's-side window rolled down about 40 percent) and a 1974 Lotus Éclat (driver's-side window rolled down about 30 percent). A 1968 VW Bus failed the test not because it didn't rough well, but because it broke down halfway through our trip to the beach.

⚠ WARNING: Solo Window Roughing is not safe. Don't do it. We suggest forming Rough Teams of two or more people per car. Have the driver wear earplugs. If at any time the driver begins to feel dizzy or disoriented, immediately adjust the window to cancel the rough. Switch positions every few minutes . . . or hours . . . or days.

ISOLATION TANKS ☺

By the second day of his historic 33-hour solo flight across the Atlantic, Charles Lindbergh grew paranoid. He felt people following him, heard voices talking to him, his skull becoming "one great eye, seeing everywhere at once." Lindbergh was sleep deprived, but more importantly, he was "sense deprived." The solitary confinement of the cockpit denied Lindbergh's brain the sensory information it needed to act normally. So, bored, his brain started entertaining itself, pulling visions, sights, and sounds from his subconscious and placing them in the waking world around him. His dreams become reality; his reality became a nightmare. Sailors and mountaineers called this phenomenon "cabin fever." HighLab calls it a good Tuesday night.

Isolation tanks provide the same sensory deprivation experience as Lindbergh's cockpit, only in a more controlled—and safer—environment. Invented in 1954 by neuro-psychiatrist John Lilly, these Jacuzzi-like chambers are filled with salt-rich water heated to our exact body temperature. A light-blocking lid seals them shut. Lilly's goal was to mute out as many senses as possible, then monitor how the brain reacts to total sensory deprivation. What he discovered was fascinating. When placed in a soundless, sightless, feeling-less environment, the brain—deprived of stimulus—would begin hallucinating during conscious states, doing all manner of crazy things to keep itself occupied. Some people in isolation tanks reported vivid waking dreams, others claimed to go out-of-body. Most reported other profound and perspective-changing events. Research into isolation tanks grew in the 1960s and 1970s but faded later in the 1980s.

Today, isolation tanks are used less for exploring altered states of consciousness and more to help people overcome psychological ailments. A 2007 study at Karlstad University in Sweden monitored 140 people suffering from stress, depression, anxiety, and chronic pain before and after sessions in an isolation tank. At the end of the study more than 75 percent of participants experienced improvement in their conditions.

Get High Now

Isolation tanks are more common than you think. Check around. Most sessions last 45 minutes. One HighLab member reported on his third session in an isolation tank to hear "one million sentient voices all scream at once." This is heavy shit.

> **Fun Fact:** *The classic (and disarmingly weird) 1980 film by Ken Russell,* Altered States, *is based on Lilly's early experiences taking psychedelic drugs in an isolation tank. Check it out.*

BEE STINGS

Bee stings for most people are painful, unpleasant experiences. For some, they can even be fatal. But for HighLab, bee stings offer a welcome psychedelic diversion to what would otherwise be a boring stroll through the woods.

Bee venom, also known as apitoxin, reacts in the body by thinning the blood, one reason it has become popular in the treatment of rheumatism. When your body senses apitoxin in the bloodstream, it begins to release cortisol and dopamine. Cortisol is a hormone produced by the adrenal gland that is only significantly present in times of discomfort or stress. Though it is often associated with negative effects such as weakened immune systems, cortisol also has positive effects. It activates the body in fight-or-flight situations, helping us to overcome our stressed situation. We have, for instance, elevated cortisol levels in our bodies after exercise.

Now, dopamine, that feel-good hormone and neurotransmitter, is released by the brain when (among other times) we are placed in new, adventurous situations in which we need our highest level of mental and physical dexterity. Like when we are stung by bees. When cortisol and dopamine couple, we get an intense feeling of satisfaction. We can even hallucinate.

The more bee stings, the more hormones and neurotransmitters are released, the higher we get. In some reported cases, people who have suffered from multiple bee stings experience a profound sense of euphoria as well as vivid illusions that can consist of altered perception of color and illuminated geometric forms. Wow.

Get High Now

Do not seek out bee stings. If you are unlucky/lucky enough to be stung by a bee (or several), take a moment out from cursing in pain to pay attention to any potential feelings of attendant euphoria. As respecters of nature, HighLab has never elicited bee stings, but rather accepts them as an occasional gift from the great god Odin. Hail bee-sting highs! Hail Odin!

FRASER SPIRAL

This illusion was created by British psychologist James Fraser, who first published it in the *British Journal of Psychology* in 1908. When you look at the Fraser Spiral it appears a single line is twisting its way into the center, spiraling into a funnel. Your eyes, Judas-like, are deceiving you. Look at it again. This time trace the "spiral" with your finger. You'll soon see the Fraser Spiral is not a "line" at all but rather a series of circles repeating in various sizes from the center.

The Fraser Spiral works by guiding the eye through a sequence of counter-angles. The eye and brain are not accustomed to processing images this geometrically complicated, and thus try to normalize the circles by imagining them as a single line, a *phantom spiral* corkscrewing its way to the center.

Get High Now

Try to follow the spiral to the center with your fingertip or a pen.
You can't. Why? 'Cuz it ain't no spiral.

BATES METHOD

Ophthalmologist William Horatio Bates, M.D. (1860–1931), believed most eye ailments—myopia, hyperopia, astigmatism, and presbyopia—were not hereditary, but caused by straining habits people unconsciously put upon their eyes. These strains, according to Bates, were the primary reason most people needed glasses and were also the cause of abnormal eye conditions such as cataracts and glaucoma.

To ease strain and improve vision, Bates developed various relaxation techniques for the eyes, calling them collectively the Bates Method. Some considered the techniques fantastic; others thought them fallacious. But everyone agreed the Bates Method made them high.

Get High Now

Because Bates believed constant exposure to light could inflict undo strain on the eyes, he suggested patients practice Palming, which he said could lull the eyes into a completely relaxed state.

Wash your hands. Sit comfortably in a chair. Close your eyes. Place your palms over your eyes without touching the eyelids. Nod your head up and down slowly and gently for ten seconds, then side to side for ten seconds. Alternate back-and-forth for one minute. When done, remove your hands and slowly open your eyes. Notice the shimmering colors, the distorted perspective. Your eyes should feel completely rested; your brain now mildly baked.

Bonus High

Find a black surface—chalkboard, paper, whatever. Stare at it closely enough so that the only thing you can see is black. Become immersed in the darkness, lose yourself in it. Stare for one minute then look away. Your vision will be clearer, colors spectral, perspective askew. Forget your glasses? You won't need them. You're high.

KUNDALINI TRANSCENDENT CHANTING ☺

Kundalini yogis follow the eleventh century Indian belief that the human body contains six or seven *chakras*, energy points that run along the human spine. They practice meditations to regulate the energy from these chakras, which they claim gives them a sense of balance, harmony, uplifted spirits . . . a wholesome, full mind-and-body high. (It might also spur blindness! See Kundalini Syndrome, page 177.)

This is a wondrous exercise that proves mystical hippie meditations can *actually* work. Be brave—give in to it. Dinner can wait.

Get High Now

Sit comfortably in an armless chair. Relax your arms to your sides. Point your forefingers towards the floor, firmly but without tensing. Curl your remaining fingers into loose fists. Now extend your thumbs out so they cover the last three fingers curled up in your hands. Close your eyes about 75 percent and focus on an imaginary point a few feet out from your nose.

Step One: Seven Minutes

Take a deep, five-second inhale through your nose, softly ballooning your stomach as you fill your lungs. As you exhale, chant in a quiet voice the mantra *Har Hare Hari Wha He Guru*. Exaggerate your mouth with each vowel. Let the phrase come out slowly; each chant should take about six seconds or so. With every exhale-chant suck your stomach into your spine—don't force it, just let it naturally curve in. It's a bit tricky at the beginning, but you'll get it. Repeat the cycle for about seven minutes.

Step Two: Two Minutes

After the verbal chanting, repeat the mantra to yourself without speaking it aloud. Listen to it in your mind.

Step Three: One Minute

You will end by concentrating three deep breaths up into your chest. Start by inhaling through your nose to a count of about five, filling up the top of your body. As you inhale, your spine should become erect but not overly tensed. When you exhale, let your body relax, your shoulders fold in a bit, head hang—become the balloon half-deflated. Repeat this two more times for a total of three breaths.

When you are ready, open your eyes. You have transcended your earthly self and are now clothed in a cloak of calmness, serenity, and good vibes that will cover you all day. Now say it one more time with us, little Krishnas: *Har Hare Hari Wha He Guru.*

TEMPORAL ALIASING BATHTUB

Imagine watching a complex action sequence in a film. Every five seconds you close your eyes for about ten seconds, then open them for another five, close for ten, and repeat. Pretty soon the action will become disjointed. For instance, you might see a man injured on the ground but will have no idea what happened to him; you'll see a car smashed into a roadblock but won't know how it got there. When fluid motion like this is chopped up into samples, a distortion of time occurs, the actions lose their comprehensible sequence. This is called Temporal Aliasing. To see this phenomenon is to glimpse into a concurrent, slower, and disjointed reality that exists side by side with our assumed fluid world. Huh? Was that a line from *The Matrix*? Could be, but no matter how overwrought the description, Temporal Aliasing offers a deeper context into how our brains perceive our actions, movies, events—everything—around us. Better, it can get us very, very high.

⚠ WARNING: Auto-Organic and Mechanical Temporal Aliasing can trigger seizures for those with photosensitive epilepsy. Use common sense: Do not attempt this exercise if you are at risk, and discontinue immediately if you feel nauseous, dizzy, or physically stressed in any way.

Get High Now

Primer for Beginners

Auto-Organic Temporal Aliasing: Open and close your eyes very quickly. While doing this look around. Try to burn into your vision the very last flash of the world before receiving the next one. Look at your hands. Look into the mirror. Look. Keep blinking. Do it for thirty seconds. This is a good way to get high when bored on a date or waiting for the bus.

For Advanced Trippers

Mechanical Temporal Aliasing: Buy a strobe light. Go into your bathroom and completely block out light from the window. (HighLab employed cardboard and duct tape.) Place the light facing the opposite wall away from any water faucets. Turn the light on—a rate of ten to fifteen flashes per second is optimum. Sit in the bathtub. The strobe light will temporarily alias everything in your vision, everything in the bathroom, making the world appear as though it has been recast in a disjointed, superslow rate. Stare. Feel.

HighLab: Getting Results

HighLab participants claimed that after five minutes in the Temporal Aliasing Bathtub, light hallucinations would occur—some of them frighteningly realistic. Most "visions" began at the source of the strobe light then grew horizontally towards the ceiling. Some members reported seeing flashes of other people in the room. If it all gets too heavy, remember that you can stop Temporal Aliasing any time by simply closing your eyes.

SHEPARD TONES ☺ 🎧

In 1964, Psychologist Roger N. Shepard experimented with stripping pitch discrimination information (the frequencies that make pitches sound either high or low) from tones and then analyzing how the brain would process these tones. He created a "pitchless" cycle of Shepard Tones and looped them over and over again. Because the tones overlap each other, and because they are missing some pitch information, escalating Shepard Tones sound as if they are continually ascending to new, higher scales. Each *preceding* Shepard Tone sounds as if it is lower than the next, while the *proceeding* tones sound higher than the last, even though we are actually just hearing a loop of the same tones over and over. It's like walking down an up-escalator—constantly moving but somehow going nowhere. If Satan made music, this is exactly what it would sound like.

Get High Now

Go to the Shepard Tones link on Gethighnow.com. Listen carefully to how the notes sound as if they are constantly climbing. Note that they, however, never seem to change key or scale. Try listening to them in descending order. They just somehow keep going down. So strange.

Fun Fact: *Super Mario 64 uses a truncated version of the Shepard Tones in the scene in which Mario is ascending the never-ending staircase.*

SOUL DANCE

This is not a James Brown-style breakdown, but a "body-spirit" dance that allows you to express your "essence" and release energies in the chakras. It's also a great way to get genuinely dirty on the dance floor.

Derived from various dance therapies first introduced in the 1940s, Soul Dance comes in many varieties, many of which are regaining popularity in modern yoga and meditation schools.

HighLab attempted three Soul Dance styles offered in San Francisco. One class asked us to close our eyes and play an imaginary instrument—and then dance with it. Another instructed us to regress to a prenatal state in a blanket on the floor. The last one wanted us to embody the spirit of our favorite animal. (This exercise spurred one member to *become* a sloth and nap in a corner until the misery was all over.) The verdict: none of these Soul Dance styles got us high, but one technique in the second class *kind of* worked for us, in much the same way I Can't Believe It's Not Butter tastes like butter. Here's how to do it.

Get High Now

Go to a quiet place in your house. Sit cross-legged on the floor. Take three very deep breaths in, each deeper than the last, one after the other without exhaling—then breathe out completely. Do this three times. Now lie on the floor, on your side in the fetal position. Return your breathing to normal and gently close your eyes. How does your body feel? Where is it uncomfortable? Think about it. After a minute or so, center your thoughts on areas of your body you *can't* feel—your organs, kidney, brain, the inside of your stomach. This centering exercise prepares your mind and body for the first "dance." Shall we?

Begin to move. Let your limbs stretch out in whichever direction feels right; loosen your torso. Don't think about it. Get up or sit down—whatever. Just move. Remove your conscious mind from your actions. Concentrate on your breath. Go deeper. Move. Feel the primitive pulse throughout your body, feel your soul take control. React without purpose, without meaning. Soon you will feel freer, stronger, more human.

PSYCHONEUROIMMUNOLOGY

Hypochondriacs feel sick because their brains are sending their bodies a *sick* message even though there is nothing physically wrong with them. The body reacts, and often times actually makes them sick. Hypochondriacs use the power of suggestion to hurt themselves. That's sad. What they should should be doing is using their thoughts to help themselves, to heal what ails them, to feel good. To get high. One way they could do this is practice some *psychoneuroimmunology*.

Combining aspects of psychology, neuroscience, behavioral medicine, and more, *psychoneuroimmunology* is the science of using our mental power to affect our body's physical condition. Before we get into how all this works, check out this study: In the mid-1970s researchers at the University of Rochester gave rats a flavored drink every day 30 minutes before giving them a drug that would suppress their immune systems. After a couple of weeks, the rats adapted by automatically suppressing their immune systems even when they were not actually given the drug that weakened their immunity. What happened was the mere *suggestion* of the drug (the flavored drink) became enough for the rats to profoundly alter their biology, for their minds to spur changes in their bodies.

The same *psychoneuroimmunology* works in humans. Our brains are in direct contact with our immune systems through neuro pathways. This is how the brain regulates our immune response (white blood cells, etc.) when we are sick or injured. When we think we are sick or injured, these immune responses can automatically kick in. After prolonged *sick* thoughts, our body will weaken and make us prone to sickness or injury, completing the vicious cycle.

Stress works the same way. A 1993 analysis of 38 studies of stressors on the human physical condition showed a consistent increase in white blood cells among various "stressed" people suffering from everything from work-related anxiety, to relationship problems, the death of a loved one, etc. These people were making themselves sick with stress.

Prolonged stress can also affect our physical ability to *ever* feel good. What happens is the constant presence of stress hormones (cortisol, for instance) can reduce the effect of good-feeling neurotransmitters like dopamine and seratonin. That means when chronically stressed-out people finally find happiness they *still* may not be able to feel physically happy—their constant stress has rewired their bodies so that they can only feel bad!

Oh God, make it stop! It's all so depressing! And we're stressing out just thinking about it! Can we please hurry up now and *get high?!*

Get High Now

According to Herbert Benson, associate professor of medicine at the Harvard Medical School, more than 60 percent of doctor visits in the United States are related to stress, most of which are poorly treated by prescription drugs, surgery, or other medical treatments. So how do we become unstressed? We think about it.

The power of suggestion is *scientifically* proven to alter our regulation of hormones, blood pressure, and more; we can use our mental process to hugely affect our physical well-being. Yes. So instead of injuring and sickening yourself with worry and negative thoughts, help yourself by thinking positive. Sure, it sounds too easy, too much like a public service message from an after-school special, but thinking good thoughts is proven to improve health, make you happy, and *high.* Meditate once a day with any number of methods in this book. Do some breathwork. Try some mystical visualization exercises. Be positive. Your life could depend on it.

MEVLEVI WHIRLING

The Sufi Dervishes of the Mevlevi order in Turkey don't whirl themselves in circles in order to get dizzy. In fact, like expertly twirling ice skaters, they don't get dizzy. They spin to see the whole of the universe, to generate a mystical current through which they serve as conduits, leaving their egos behind in their pursuit of the *kemal*—the "perfect."

Get High Now

Find an open space, preferably outdoors. Push yourself clockwise with your left foot. Keep your right foot on the ground and use it to center yourself. Hold your arms out. Point the fingers on your right hand skyward; this allows you to access gifts from heaven. Point downward the fingers on your left hand; this filters the light through you and down to the earth. Spin. After a few moments—or minutes—put both feet on the ground and stop. A gossamer cloak of colors spins around you. Kemal. You are the light.

ROSEMARY

Take six ounces of rosemary tops, two pints of spirits or wine, let sit for four days, and what do you get? A cure for lame limbs. So thought Elizabeth, Queen of Hungary, who championed this concoction she called Hungary Water in the fourteenth century as a quick fix for paralysis, gout, and all manner of other ailments.

Elizabeth wasn't alone. Rosemary has been used for centuries around the world to relieve headaches, anxiety, and infections, and as a memory restorer. It still is. In 2003, a study conducted by the Human Cognitive Neuroscience Unit at the University of Northumbria, Newcastle, U.K., tested the memory-restorative effects of rosemary on 145 participants. Groups were placed in cubicles scented with either rosemary or lavender, or no odor. Those exposed to rosemary experienced "significant enhancement of performance for overall quality of memory." (Paradoxically, they also experienced slower speed of recall when compared to other groups.)

Some scientists have attributed rosemary's memory-boosting ability to its carnosic acid, which has been proven effective in protecting the brain from free radicals and even lowering the risk of strokes, Alzheimer's, and Lou Gehrig's disease, a.k.a. amyotrophic lateral sclerosis, a degenerative disease that attacks the central nervous system, and has disabled British physicist Stephen Hawking.

OK, so improving your memory and immune system is cool, but can rosemary really get you high? Ask the Evenks, the indigenous people of Northern China and Russia who prefer the narcotic effects of the smoked leaves of the herb over ingesting hallucinogenic mushrooms. Additionally, according to legend, rosemary was also responsible for spurring Norse Vikings into pillaging berserker frenzies! Convinced yet?

Get High Now

HighLab knows nothing of smoking rosemary and does not condone the practice, though we do condone going berserker—and playing Atari's *Berserk*—whenever possible. Further, some of us come from English stock and enjoy a cup o' tea in the afternoon. To this tea we add a few sprigs of rosemary. We like it for its calming, mildly numbing effect. You might also. Take a small handful of rosemary and put it in some boiling water for a few minutes. Cover with a lid. Strain the rosemary and drink to your health, memory, and going berserk.

⚠ Warning: If you are allergic to rosemary, don't ingest rosemary.

> **Fun Fact:** *In the same 2003 Newcastle study, exposure to lavender produced "significant decrement in performance of working memory" as well as impaired reaction times of memory performance for test subjects. Feeling dumb? Try replacing your girlfriend's artisanal handmade French lavender soap in the shower.*

CORIANDER

A popular Iranian folk remedy for anxiety and insomnia, the fruit of the annual herb coriander (whose leaves are known as cilantro), in the right doses, offers aggressive psychoactive effects and produces all manner of hilarity and good times—just before it makes you violently ill.

A few years ago some hippies spilled a 50-quart barrel of coriander oil in the storage warehouse of a health food distributor. The fumes immediately sent the crew into bouts of uncontrollable laughter and reverie. Wild hallucinations followed. (Yes!) Hours later things turned violent; the longhairs grew irritable, irrational, and angry, lurching pitbull-like at one another. (No!) The next day, all suffered from extreme nausea. Sounds insane, right? Not really. You can view an exact replica of coriander intoxication at most frat bars on any given Friday night—minus perhaps the citrus-sweet coriander scent.

Get High Now

In small doses, coriander helps remedy stomach troubles like flatulence and diarrhea, and has been used in Asia for hundreds of years as a treatment for measles. In larger doses, well . . . HighLab has no desire to become irrational, or angry, or violently ill, and neither should you. However, we do enjoy international cuisine, so we threw a few tablespoons of coriander into our curry one night. No hallucinations or hilarity were reported but the next morning we couldn't help but remember the fourth line in Act III of *Hamlet*, where the young prince soliloquizes over Polonius's dead body: *Why Indian food, why do you tempt us with your deliciousness at night and always scorch thee bum in the morning?*

BINAURAL BEATS

When two tones of specific frequencies are played through headphones, the brain can become confused and produce its own, imagined tone—a three-dimensional audio hallucination heard only within the head of the listener. The frequencies that produce this phenomenon are known as Binaural Beats.

What is happening is that the brain is not used to hearing frequencies in each ear so close together and with such intensity— these sounds do not occur in nature and so no mechanism in our brains has evolved to understand them. Instead, the *superior olivary nucleus*, the area of the brain that controls aspects of three-dimensional sound perception, bridges the difference between the varying frequencies in Binaural Beats with a common "third tone" in an attempt to normalize this audio into something we can understand. When we hear this "third tone" it sounds as if it were not coming from the external audio signal, not from the ears, but from *somewhere else*—disappearing and reappearing in the front and back of the head. What's weirder is that each person hears the "third tone" differently: People with Parkinson's disease can't hear it at all; women will hear different tones as they move through their menstrual cycle.

Binaural Beats were discovered in 1839 by Prussian physicist Heinrich Wilhelm Dove (1803–1879), but they didn't gain much public interest until the early 1970s. Then, scientist Gerald Oster postulated that the brain wasn't solely affected by Binaural Beats. He tested this theory with fMRIs and found he was right. The neurological system as well as other parts of the body responded to the frequencies.

Since Oster's discovery, Binaural Beats have been used as cure-alls for everything from impotence to bulimia. Spurious, right? Sure, but the difference between Binaural Beats, and, say, magic healing crystals, is that Binaural Beats have been clinically shown to *physically* affect the listener's brain and body, even triggering the pituitary gland to flood the body with good-feeling hormones like dopamine. In other words, Binaural Beats are proven to get us mentally, physically, physiologically, biologically, scientifically, inextricably high. What are you waiting for?

Get High Now

Grab some headphones and go to Gethighnow.com. Though not necessary, consider sitting comfortably on a couch or bed, dimming the lights, and closing your eyes while listening to the tracks. This will help dampen your other senses and allow you to better concentrate on the audio. Remember that people hear Binaural Beats differently, and some may have trouble hearing the "third tone" at all. Try it for at least five minutes.

Binaural Beats worked for every HighLab member, ladies and gentlemen alike. We all thought it one of the most dazzling audio highs in this amazing book. Have fun.

MOTH LARVA

While on one of his many travels through South America in the early 1800s, French botanist Augustin de Saint-Hilaire gathered a staggering 24,000 specimens of plants and 16,000 insects, all the while contracting a handful of tropical diseases. He also recorded culinary oddities of the indigenous cultures through which he traveled, not least of which was a tradition of the Mailalis, a tribe in the southwestern Brazilian province of Minas Gerais. The Mailalis ate moth larvae to get high.

Known as *bicho de taquara*, the larva belonged to the Myelobia genus of moth. There are twenty-four species of Myelobia throughout South America, plus one in Mexico and one in Guatemala. The larvae, or grubs, of this species feed on common bamboos and can grow to (a disgusting) four inches long. According to the Mailalis, munching a dried *bicho*—sans the head, which they considered poisonous—will induce an ecstatic sleep filled with all manner of psychedelic visions that could last more than a day.

Saint-Hilaire himself became a fan, if not for the high of the Myelobia larva than at least for its flavor. He wrote in an 1824 journal, (translated) "In spite of my repugnance, I followed the example of the young savage [who removed the head and intestinal tube of the larva, and sucked out the soft, whitish substance which remained in the skin] and found, in this strange food, an extremely agreeable flavor which recalled that of the most delicate cream." *Delicate cream!*

Get High Now

The adult Myelobia moth emerges in September, which means the larva reaches its maximize size July through August. This is the time larvaheads should get slurping. Though the Mailalis tribe were long ago overrun, the larva they so regaled remains. Next summer, hop a plane to Brazil's Tancredo Neves/Confins International Airport, grab a cab, and yell to the driver, "Bamboo grubs or bust, Berto." Then hold on.

GANZFELD ANOMALOUS INFORMATION TRANSFER 👥 👂

The way in which scientists working for the U.S. military tested subjects for psychic ability in the 1970s was through Ganzfeld Anomalous Information Transfer. In this intensely weird exercise, one subject—the Receiver—sat in a dim red-lit room with ping-pong ball halves over his eyes and headphones tuned to static. These props were believed to mute the Receiver's senses, making him more receptive to paranormal suggestion. All the while, another subject—the Sender—sat in an electromagnetically shielded and/or soundproofed room trying to send a "target" to the Receiver through extrasensory perception (ESP). Most Ganzfeld tests lasted a half hour, after which the Receiver would be shown a card with four "target" images and asked to choose the one sent by the Sender.

In a 1983 study conducted at the Psychophysical Research Laboratories, consisting of 354 trials, the success rate of direct hits (the Receiver guessing the exact card target sent by the Sender) was 34 percent. In a related study in 1985, the hit rate was 37 percent. These results are not too impressive considering the 25 percent success rate of a random guess. But in a later 1985 study of twenty Juilliard School (of contemporary performing arts) students, the hit rate jumped dramatically to 50 percent. Musicians in the group scored an impressive 75 percent hit rate. Some researchers inferred that individuals with artistic and musical ability are more naturally gifted with ESP powers . . . or just lucky bullshitters.

Though 40 percent of Americans today claim to believe in ESP, scientific proof of the phenomenon remains inconclusive. That shouldn't stop you from trying the Ganzfeld Anomalous Information Transfer—which for every member of HighLab offered a wholly mind-expanding and at times hallucinatory high.

Get High Now

Grocery List:

- Two participants
- A ping-pong ball, cut in half
- Scotch tape
- Headphones
- A red light bulb

Prepare the Receiver: Ganzfeld Anomalous Information Transfer requires that the Receiver be in a state of mild sensory deprivation. To induce this, find a flat surface on which the Receiver can lay undisturbed: floor, couch, bed, or inversion table. Place a lamp containing the red light bulb a few feet from the Receiver's face. Go to Gethighnow.com and cue up pink or white noise. Place headphones over the Receiver's ears. Adhere a couple strips of Scotch tape to two sides of each ping-pong ball half. The halves should fit comfortably over the eyes, with the Scotch tape holding them lightly to the face. When comfortable, begin the audio.

The ping-pong ball halves will allow the Receiver muted visual details of the outside world, enough to evoke the imagination but not enough to cause a distraction. The Pink Noise at Gethighnow.com will mute out all exterior sounds and lull the brain into a state receptive to ESP.

Prepare the Sender: Once the Receiver is in a receptive state (noise playing, red light on), the Sender should go to another room where she cannot hear or see the Receiver. She will choose one of five Zener cards (below) on which to concentrate. Sender should concentrate on the *feel* and *context* of the symbol, not the literal shape. For instance, if the Sender chooses an O, she should imagine a bicycle wheel, top, merry-go-round or other circular, spinning objects.

At the end of thirty minutes, the Sender joins the Receiver. Receiver removes the ping-pong ball halves and headphones, turns off the red light, and immediately writes down on paper the strongest images he imagined while *receiving*. The Sender should remain silent, and need not continue to concentrate on the target symbol. After the Receiver has written down notes, the Sender reveals the target on the card on which she was concentrating.

Sender and Receiver can then switch roles if desired.

Fun Fact: *The 1970s were a banner decade for extrasensory perception. Not only were parapsychologists wowing the bushy-haired audience of* That's Incredible *every week, they were also rooting out communist missile bases from Leningrad (now St. Petersburg) to Africa. The CIA and the U.S. military were so inspired by psychic research that they created the Stargate Project, one of a number of federally funded ESP testing labs. At its peak, Stargate had as many as 14 labs researching ESP, with over 22 active military and domestic "viewers" providing data. One viewer was asked to scan military threats around the world. He identified the exact location of the* USS Stark *frigate in the Persian Gulf on May 17, 1987. In a 1972 study, a viewer in a sealed-off room was able to read a five-digit number in another room. The viewer got every number correct (the odds of guessing the number are 1:99,999). Though Stargate had successes early on, interest in ESP waned in the late 1980s. In 1995 the U.S. military finally pulled the plug. And to think the psychics never saw it coming.*

FINGER PHALLUS

Stone records show the Penuu Phingier (Phingerus Phalus) was used as early as the 3rd century B.C. by Egyptian priests in fertility rituals before the annual wheat harvest. In some of the most majestic and awe-inspiring ceremonies in Egyptian culture, hundreds of thousands of Egyptians stood upon the exterior limestone ground-level steps of the Pyramid of Cheops and positioned their hands in the Penuu Phingier, chanting *nefit redi* "grow, Phingiers, grow."

Later, in the first century B.C., Roman Emperor Tiberius adopted the cherished finger gestures, changing its name to Phingerus Phalus, and used the hand position in his own "fertility rituals" with sentries around the court.

Note: Facts from the above description were taken from Wikepydia.org, a Russia-based Web site that has since been taken offline for posting egregiously false information and ridiculously lame history-based jokes.

Get High Now

Make two fists. Hold them about 8 inches from your eyes. Extend the index finger from each hand so that they just touch each other. Concentrate on the spot where the fingers touch. Now, focus your eyes on the distance behind your fingers. Relax your vision. Let it go. Gently separate your fingers a quarter-inch. Do this back and forth.

Play with the Finger Phallus. Go ahead. It's not dirty. Move your fingers closer to your eyes. Separate your fingers and watch it float. Watch it grow. *Nefti redi.*

DISAPPEARING NOISE ☺

The human ear processes frequencies between 20 Hz (low sounds) and 20 kHz (high sounds). Though we cannot hear above around 20 kHz, other animals can. Dogs, for instance, can hear frequencies up to 40 kHz; a mouse can hear up to about 90 kHz. Canine audio trainers and rodent repellents exploit these aural ranges, emitting high frequencies that are silent to humans yet highly annoying to other animals.

While we cannot hear frequencies out of the 20 kHz range, we can sometimes *feel* them, or rather, we can *feel* their absence. Japanese sound artist Ryoki Ikeda developed such a frequency and featured it on his insane album titled +/-. HighLab audio technicians have created our own version below.

Get High Now

HighLab Black Noise Disappearer Frequency ranges just at the human frequency threshold. When you click the audio track on Gethighnow.com don't expect to hear anything—but don't turn it off. Let the track finish, let the "silence" play out. When the track ends you'll notice a different silence is apparent. Try it on your stereo speakers as well. Turn the volume to LOUD, play the track. Try to listen for when it stops. It's an indescribable experience. Not necessarily a good experience, just indescribable.

> **Fun Fact:** *What's an "Hz"? It's an abbreviation for Hertz, the International System of Units base of frequency, and refers to cycles of sound per second. Think of sound like a vinyl record, your ear as the needle. When you play a record on a turntable at a low speed, the grooves in the record are read by the needle at a slower rate and the music sounds lower in pitch. Alternately, when you play a record at high speed, the needle reads the grooves more quickly and the pitch gets*

higher. The human ear works in the same way. Instead of record grooves, the ear processes waves of pressure fluctuation. When air pressure in the ear is fluctuating slowly (a slower cycle-per-second, or Hertz) we hear it as lower pitch; when air pressure fluctuates more quickly in our ears we perceive it as a higher pitch. Further, the level of air pressure in our ears—the amplitude—determines how loud we hear the sound.

THE PERICOPES OF HENRY II

Backstabbing was a rite of passage in olden days. It kept kingdoms in constant flux by provided otherwise low-caste society members the opportunity to overthrow their leaders for any reason, at any time. The Holy Roman Emperor Henry II (973–1024) was all too conscious of this fact. One way he protected himself was to secure his circle of allies in the church with a strict law of celibacy. Being celibate meant that his bishop friends would never have children, and thus Henry would never have to worry about a bishop's heir coming to power and challenging his rule. When a bishop died, his office and land would simply be redirected back to Henry, who could choose another cohort to take it all over.

The strategy worked. Henry ruled as King of Italy from 1002 and King of Germany from 1004 until his death in 1024. He was eventually canonized as a saint in 1146.

Henry II was not only a shrewd politician but a lover of the arts. Around 1002 he commissioned a lavishly illuminated manuscript, *The Pericopes of Henry II*. Among other fantastical biblical representations, *Pericopes* featured the first known visual illusion, the first-ever illustrated visual high.

Get High Now

The page "Madonna and Child" features a (guess what) Madonna and child seated in the center of three Corinthian columns. At the top, all columns appear to be constructed in-line at the same horizontal plane; however, below we see that the base of the columns is triangulated. The combined effect creates a disorientation in depth. The Liuthar circle of illuminators who drafted the image tried to place the Madonna at center without bothering to align the visual perspective. And looking at this trippy illustration a thousand years later, we commend them on a job done well. See a larger image of the *Pericopes* at Gethighnow.com.

SNAKE BREATH

Some yogis believe breathing like a snake can infuse your mind and body with primitive, serpentine energy. But how, you ask, is breathing like a snake any different from breathing like any other reptile? Well, for one, snakes usually prey on animals larger than their mouths. This requires them to extend their trachea (the tube used to fill the lungs with air) below the prey to create a hole in which they can inhale and exhale air. With each breath, snakes rest from a few seconds to as long as a few minutes as their elongated right lung processes the oxygen into their bloodstreams. Some snakes have a smaller left lung; a few even have a third lung that runs along the trachea.

This lung orientation is specific only to snakes, giving them a breathing style uniquely their own. When humans breathe like snakes, we can devolve our physiology to the Squamata order of our reptile cousins, feeling in our veins the same cold blood that courses in theirs. This gives us a focused energy boost and a creepy, crawly high.

Get High Now

Sit comfortably on the floor or in a chair. Put the tip of your tongue between your front teeth so that it sticks slightly out of your lips. Take a breath in through your mouth to a count of about three, feeling the air *hiss* past your lips and teeth. Make a hissing sound. Exhale at the same speed through the sides of your mouth hissing all the way. While breathing try to tuck in your stomach as you exhale; extend the stomach as you inhale.

Now breathe very deeply to a count of five or even ten, filling up your lungs completely as you hiss. Hold your breath for as long as you can, then exhale slowly back through your mouth, continuing to hold your tongue with your teeth. Be sure not to let the air burst out; let it slowly diffuse from your lungs, let it *hiss* out of you. Try squinting your eyes a bit—become the serpent. Repeat at least twenty times, or more if you feel like it. HighLab found this an excellent exercise for men to practice while standing next to other men at a public urinal. *Sssssssssst.*

SLEEP DEPRIVATIONS

In 1964, seventeen-year-old Randy Gardner set the then-record for sleeplessness by staying awake for eleven straight days. Within two days of going without sleep, he was experiencing vivid hallucinations, mild paranoia, and other random coolness. The longer he stayed awake, the more these delusions increased. On the eleventh day of sleeplessness, Gardner was asked by a doctor supervising him to count down from 100 in increments of seven. Gardner made it to number 65 then stopped. The doctor asked why he stopped. Gardner looked at him blankly and said he had totally forgotten what he was doing.

Most of us who have lasted more than a day without sleep are familiar with the mild auditory hallucinations and visual "tracing" that occurs. Consider that these effects usually double within 48 hours, then triple thereafter. It's so effective that in the past two thousand years numerous religions from Christianity to Islam have also incorporated sleeplessness into their worship as a means to get closer to God.

Get High Now

There are a surprisingly large number of recreational sleep-deprivers online, most of whom have developed their own methods of keeping themselves awake and now have time to spend all night writing ranty blogs about it. If you haven't done it in a while, try staying up for at least 24 hours some weekend night. Notice the changes to visual and audio perception. The longest a HighLab member ever made it was about 36 hours of sleeplessness, after which time she had to retire to bed—not because she was tired, but because she was so absolutely freaked out by all the flashing and popping visual and audio hallucinations she was experiencing. If she went on longer, the effects would only increase. When it comes to sleep deprivation, it's easy. Any method will work. Just don't sleep.

⚠ WARNING: While short-term sleep deprivation has been shown to have few if any known aftereffects, long-term deprivations can be detrimental to health and have been linked to diabetes, headaches, hypertension, loss of memory, nausea, decreased sexual appetite, depression, and more. Not sleeping also checks you in to the "hobo salon," where customers come out looking not hot, but raccoon-eyed, perma-smiling, with ratty hair and clammy skin. Don't make it a habit.

If you stay awake more than 24 hours, plan on your sleeping recovery time to be about 10 hours; the longer you deprive yourself, the longer you'll need. After his 11 days of sleeplessness, Gardner slept 14 hours, woke up and felt refreshed, stayed awake 24 hours, then resumed his normal 8-hour-a-night schedule. Recovery times vary. Save it for a long weekend.

GIRAFFE LIVER

Sudan is the largest country in Africa and the tenth largest country in the world. Sudan has giraffes, lots of them. People in Sudan, such as the Humr tribe of Baggara Arabs, like drinks. They like giraffes. They like making drinks from giraffes. And from these giraffe drinks they get high.

Humrs hunt giraffes for their livers and bone marrow, from which they make a traditional beverage called *umm nyolokh*. A cup or two of *umm nyolokh*, they claim, induces a wild, hallucinatory high filled with vivid, waking dreams.

Author Richard Rudley describes how, in the 1950s, anthropologist Ian Cunnison joined the Humrs in a hunting expedition to make *umm nyolokh*. Cunnison claimed after ingesting the drinks, Humrs experienced waking dream-visions, typically featuring the giraffe. Though Cunnison thought the effects of *umm nyolokh* to be self-provoked, Rudley argues the bone marrow of the giraffe could be full of DMT, the naturally occurring psychoactive found in many hallucinogenic plants and animals. (Humans also contain DMT; see Schizophrenic Blood, page 75). Either way, the Humrs are hooked, claiming once you've drunk the *umm nyolokh,* you "will return to giraffe again and again."

Get High Now

Procure fresh giraffe liver and bone marrow. Blend. Drink. Hallucinate. Repeat.

VOMIT VECTORS

Look at this illusionary high (following page). The dots appear to be moving, undulating and animated. Some researchers blame our neurons—the brain and body's messenger cells. When the neurons process a white area from our eyes, they send an on/off signal to our brains. Black areas generate the opposite off/on signal. The complex map of black and white areas in Vomit Vectors overloads our brains by countering on/off with off/on signals.

Usually when the brain receives countering on/off and off/on signals like this it is because either a) the area in which the eyes are focusing is flashing, such as what happens when lights turn on and off; or b) objects are in motion, such as what happens when we watch, say, an ant crawl across a white piece of paper, an area of focus once black with the ant then turns white as the ant moves forward.

OK, so our brains process Vomit Vectors as changing flashing on/off and off/on. Fine. But then we realize the illustration is *not* really flashing—it's an illustration printed on a piece of paper. Our brains rule this "flashing" option out. With no other logical choice, the brain has to assume Vomit Vectors as moving. And so, just like that, these two-dimensional unanimated objects create a perception of motion.

It's complicated, and the above is hybridized HighLab theory culled from way too many insanely detailed sources—we read all this crap so you won't have to. Though why and how this illusionary high works is still somewhat of a mystery, *where* it works is not: It's in your stomach. Because after five minutes of gazing at this you might want to vomit. Give it a try.

Get High Now

Stare at Vomit Vectors for at least one minute—longer if you can stomach it. Disgusting.

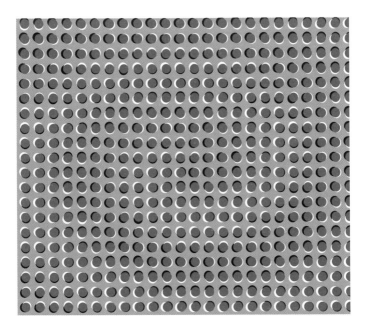

SUDARSHAN KRIYA ☺

Sudarshan Kriya is a form of breathwork discovered by Sri Sri Ravi Shankar (*not* the Beatles' sitarist, but the modern-day meditation guru) during a ten-day meditation he underwent in 1982. Shankar believed that by practicing one's *kriya*, one could saturate the mind and body with calming, positive energy. Studies published in *Biological Psychology: The Annals of the New York Academy of Sciences* and other medical journals show Sudarshan Kriya is indeed very effective in reducing stress, depression, and other maladies as well as boosting immune functions. HighLab can say without a doubt (and without any sarcasm) that Sudarshan Kriya is a totally immersive, powerful exercise with immediate and intense whole-mind/body benefits. It feels great.

Various yoga and meditation disciplines offer various forms of *kriya*. While the techniques of each *kriya* may vary, all share the same underlying goal: to awaken within the mind and body *kundalini* energy, the "cosmic force" that yogis believe lies within the *chakras* of the spine.

Special Note: Consider the following Sudarshan Kriya exercise a mere teaser of the full kriya *exercise. If earnestly interested in Sudarshan Kriya, we suggest you investigate Sri Sri's courses, which are taught at schools throughout the world.*

Get High Now

Sit in a chair or on the ground with your back against a wall. Make sure your back is supported and that you are comfortable. Close your eyes. Breathing only through your nose, take a deep breath and pull air down to the pit of your abdomen. Extend your belly as you breathe in, and retract it as you breathe out. Take two more breaths in this manner; then begin the cycle below:

Step One: Inhale slowly and deeply to the count of *five*, and exhale completely to the count of *five*. Do this ten times.

Step Two: Inhale more quickly to the count of *three*, making sure you breathe in completely, filling your lungs down to your abdomen. Exhale completely to the count of *three*. Do this ten times.

Step Three: Inhale still more quickly now, filling the lungs with just a count of *one*; exhale quickly and aggressively to the count of *one*. Really push the air in and out; fill and empty your lungs completely with each inhale/exhale. Do this fifteen times. Go back to slow breaths (**Step One**) and repeat the entire cycle two more times for a total of three full cycles.

When you've finished, lie down on the floor and let your breathing return to normal. Stay there for a minute or two. Then open your eyes.

FACE OFF ◉

Faces. They are the first thing we begin to recognize as a child, how we distinguish our friends, family, and coworkers, how we view ourselves. We look at them every day, monitor them for reactions, stare at them everywhere we go. Our minds get so accustomed to processing and reading faces that we become hardwired to see face-like characteristics in objects that actually aren't faces. We make faces out of clouds, stained shrouds, and cheese sandwiches. We even make faces out of faces.

Get High Now

We were going to suggest for this high that you place a mask on a rod and tie it to a slow-playing turntable, but then realized nobody would do that. And those who would actually do it should be spending their time doing something else, like changing out of their sweatpants and returning this long overdue book to the library.

When you click on Face Off at Gethighnow.com the image you will see is a video of a mask spinning slowly in a circle. As the mask turns inside-out, the inverse face-image appears to be turning the other way. There are no shadows in this image to cue us, so our brains rely on what little information they have to make sense of the image. Because we are so used to seeing faces in a particular way—particularly *not* seeing faces inversed as they are in the video—we interpret the inverse mask image as not inside-out, but just spinning in the opposite direction. It's a simple yet baffling thing to behold. So behold!

> **Fun Fact**: *The* fusiform gyrus *is a part of the temporal lobe towards the front of the brain that handles how we see and understand color, words, numbers, abstractions, and faces. When the fusiform gyrus gets disrupted, some researchers believe it can inhibit our ability to recognize faces. The disorder* prosopagnosia—*"face blindness," in which a person has full mental capacity but cannot recognize faces no matter how many times he sees them—is believed to be related to malfunctioning in the fusiform gyrus.*

HALLUCINOGENIC-PLANT-INFUSED HONEY

The curative benefits of honey have been known for millennia—and so have the psychotropic effects. Xenophon, a Greek soldier from around 400 B.C., wrote about the buzz a batch of "mad" honey had on soldiers, first wasting them into oblivion, then poisoning them. It wasn't the honey itself that stoned these soldiers, it was the plants from which the bees made it. When bees harvest nectar from the flowers of hallucinogenic plants, traces of the hallucinogen are transferred to the bee honeycomb, which is transferred to the honey, which is ingested by soldiers. Who get high.

Get High Now

Wild honey harvested near outcroppings of locoweed, oleander, thorn apple, mountain laurel, as well as other psychotropic plants like morning glory, marijuana, and poppies has a much higher chance of producing hallucinogenic honey. Grab a *Farmers' Almanac*, U-Haul, and relocate now!

WAGON WHEELING

This is the visual high that occurs when a rotating spoked wheel appears to be either stopped or spinning in the opposite direction from which it is actually traveling. Many of us have noticed it in old western films or on television. In these media, the phenomenon that creates the Wagon Wheel effect is called *temporal aliasing* (page 37)—an illusion that happens when the sampling rate of a particular medium overlaps incongruously with the rate of a spinning object.

Consider that film spins about 24 frames per second; television broadcasts at around 60 frames per second. When the sampling rate (frames per second) of these media can't keep up with the sampling rate (rotation of the spokes) of the wagon wheel, the wheel becomes temporally aliased. Wagon Wheeling is exaggerated and altered depending on which media you view it in.

The Reason Wagon Wheels Look Stationary in Movies and TV

Imagine looking at an analog clock. Both hands are locked at 12:00 sharp. If you close your eyes for exactly twelve hours then open them, the hands look as though they have not moved, although twelve hours have passed. The same principle affects the spinning wagon wheel on television or in the movies. The wheel appears stationary even when it is moving forward because the frames of the film or television are opening and shutting at a rate *perfectly synched* with spinning spokes of the wagon wheel. It's just like opening your eyes every twelve hours when looking at that analog clock, but thousands of times faster.

The Reason Wagon Wheels Appear to Run Backwards in Movies and TV

Again, imagine you are looking at an analog clock. Both hands are locked at 12:00 sharp. If you close your eyes for exactly eleven hours then open them, both hands will be locked in at 11:00 sharp. Close them for another eleven hours and the hands will be locked at 10:00, and so on. Even though time was moving forward eleven hours at a time, what you view are the hands of the clock moving slowly backwards, one hour at a time. Time seems to be reversing. This same phenomenon explains the wagon wheel's backwards appearance on television or the movies. How quickly the wheel appears to be moving backwards depends on the ratio of speed of the spokes to the frames-per-second rate of the media.

Now, How Wagon Wheeling Can Make You High

You don't have to watch westerns to Wagon Wheel. In a 1967 article for *Nature*, W. A. H. Rushton of the University of Cambridge Physiological Laboratory discovered that continuous humming could create a vibration in the eyes that could mimic in real life the temporal aliasing effect of a wagon wheel spinning on film or television. Rushton knew that sound vibrations will move at quicker speeds with higher pitch, so he concentrated on a spinning object with spoke-like features (the lugnuts of a car rim, for instance) and started humming very low and then higher until the frequency of his hum matched the spinning rate of the lugnuts of the car. That's when a temporal aliasing effect occurred, and the object Wagon Wheeled. Once aliased, Rushton altered the pitch to make the spinning object appear as though it were slowing, reversing, or stationary, even though it was continuing to move forward at the same rate.

Get High Now

Next time you're a passenger in a car, check out the rims of other cars traveling parallel to you. Begin humming a single, low tone. If no Wagon Wheeling effect occurs, increase the pitch of your hum slowly. Keep watching the rims of the cars. With a little luck you'll see them Wagon Wheeling. Once you see the effect, slightly lower or raise the pitch of your hum and notice how the rims *alias*, moving quicker, slower, or even appearing as though they are stopping altogether.

A vibrating mirror can also produce a Wagon Wheel. While riding in a passenger seat (do not ever attempt while driving), direct the rear-view mirror to the rims of cars traveling alongside. If the vibrations of your car and the rims of the surrounding cars alias in just the right speeds, you'll see some very weird Wagon Wheeling.

Fun Fact: *Ever noticed the weird flickering bars that show up on the screens of computers or televisions when they are shown in the background of TV news segments or video? Or have you ever focused a video camera on a turned-on computer screen or television? Then you've seen it: that flashing screen of light, that astral portal to another dimension. What is happening is the video camera is operating at a sampling rate (frame-per-second) counter to that of the computer or television. The result is an illusion similar to blinking quickly at a strobe light: Sometimes the light appears on, sometimes it appears off. This is another example of temporal aliasing. If only the world could look like that all the time.*

Bonus High

If you use an older computer monitor (with a cathode ray tube) wave an open hand in front of it. Whoa! You'll see your hand caught in a psychedelic strobe-effect in front of the screen. That's because cathode ray monitors work like film projectors, flashing an image onto the screen at a "refresh rate" between about 60 and 90 Hz. When you wave an open hand in front of it, the monitor becomes aliased by the moving fingers; the moving fingers "strobe" our view of the monitor like frames in a film strip. Since the fingers operate at a sampling rate counter to that of the monitor's refresh rate, your hand becomes temporally aliased in front of the monitor. You've created your own little Wagon Wheel!

GLOSSOLALIA

On the evening of December 31, 1899, Agnes Ozman asked her preacher to lay his hands on her and fill her body with the light of the Lord. When he did, she barked—she bumbled, slurred, and coughed out words in a language never before spoken, never before heard. It was a language wholly her own. Ozman's experience was so revelatory thousands soon were speaking in their own personal languages. And thus was the founding of the first Pentecostal church in the United States, the sect of Christianity that practices the ancient art of *glossolalia*, or speaking in tongues.

Christians aren't the only ones to practice glossolalia. For thousands of years pagans, shamans, Hindus, and others have spoken in tongues to get high.

Get High Now

For Pentecostals, glossolalia is easy; they simply open their "souls" and let "the spirit" speak through them. Try it. Forget language. Forget comprehension. Let what is in you step out. Start vocalizing unselfconsciously whatever comes to mind: syllables, tones, moans, repetitions. Do it aloud. We all have our own tongue. Speak it for five minutes. It feels liberating—and sounds really creepy.

> **Fun Fact:** *In 2006, researchers at the University of Pennsylvania recorded the brain images of five women practicing glossolalia. All showed the same pattern. While in glossolalia, the parts of the brain that usually control language as well as the thinking centers were all relatively muted, whereas the areas that control self-consciousness were not. The study showed that glossolalia induced not a trance, not a language process, but some kind of other, unexplained state of consciousness. One woman in the study described the feeling: "You're not really out of control. But you have no control over what's happening. You're just flowing. You're in a realm of peace and comfort, and it's a fantastic feeling."*

NUTMEG (Do Not Do It)

Don't believe your mama; nutmeg isn't just for eggnog. Trippers worldwide have been ripped on this bitter spice for thousands of years. As early as the first century B.C., Vedic Indians used the nut—actually it is the seed of the myristica evergreen tree—as a cure for everything from headaches to bad breath. The popularity of nutmeg as a recreational high grew when Portuguese traders introduced it to Europeans in the fifteenth century. Slaves chomped on it on long-distance voyages to stave off pain and seasickness. Jazz saxophonist Charlie "Yardbird" (his nickname before becoming "Bird") Parker was a big fan, giving nutmeg out to his bandmates before shows. In 1947, Malcolm X was introduced to it while in jail, claiming a "penny matchbox" full of nutmeg had the kick of "three or four reefers."

What keeps 'meggers coming back for more is the large amounts of myristicin, an organic compound in nutmeg that if taken in the quantities of 10 to 30 grams provokes intense hallucinations, visual distortions, mild euphoria, peripheral flashes, and other psychoactive effects. These effects can last for up to twelve hours. Quantities greater than your body can handle lead to nutmeg toxicity, which can result in thought disorder, shakiness, and general sweaty, clammy misery.

Get High (Not)

HighLab never ingested nutmeg. We may be dumb (yet handsome) but we do not have a death wish. One HighLab member recalled hearing about a kid in high school who on Christmas Eve snuck into the kitchen shelf and gobbled a few teaspoons of nutmeg intended for the evening eggnog. He went quickly asleep and woke up ten hours later feeling like Paula Abdul: incoherent, dizzy, unable to string words together or navigate depth perception—totally and utterly useless. He swore off 'megging forever after. Do Not Do It.

SENSORY OVERLOAD

Almost every meditation high requires us to relax and remove superfluous thoughts from the mind. Even though meditation can change your life, HighLab knows some of you won't ever attempt it. Maybe you "have trouble concentrating," or "can't sit still for thirty minutes," or "don't have the time," or "get jittery." Whatever. You know who you are. And for you impatient souls, we offer Sensory Overload.

The opposite of sensory deprivation (page 91), the point of this therapy is to stimulate as many senses as harshly and as quickly as possible—to clog the brain with so much stimuli that it eventually blows out, leaving the overloadee in a temporarily altered state of consciousness. As little as a fifteen-minute session of Sensory Overload can induce a psychedelic stupor; longer episodes can evoke out-of-body experiences.

Get High Now

There are as many ways to overstimulate someone into a trance as there are ways to fry an egg. That is, there are about three. The method below worked for HighLab.

Grocery List:

- Four people
- Two forks
- Computer Headset
- Smelling salts or Cajun pepper
- Laptop computer

Set up a laptop computer on the floor and go to Gethighnow.com. Have the overloadee lie on the floor facing the computer screen, headphones on. The other three participants should be surrounding him on all sides, one person holding the smelling salts, one holding two forks, the other hovering. To begin, start the Sensory Overload audio and visual track. As the overloadee's ears and eyes are assaulted by the streaming montage, the forker should lightly and unpredictably stab the leg and knee area; someone else will waft smelling salts periodically in front of the overloadee's nose. The last person should rotate around calling the overloadee's name, lightly kicking his sides, and creating general havoc. Do this for at least ten minutes, or as long as long as it takes for the overloadee to get totally overloaded.

POSITIVE AFTERIMAGES

A surprisingly large number of quasi-mystics in the last decade have taken up the art of "sungazing" as a means to elevate the consciousness and heal themselves of all that ails. One guy in Maryland has spent the last twenty years staring at the noonday sun for thirty minutes a day.

Beyond perhaps the "thrill" of risking permanent blindness, this guy and his fellow solar psychos are attracted to sungazing for the positive afterimage. After prolonged staring at the bright light of the sun, the photoreceptors in the eyes get lazy; they stop processing the image of the sun, and start *automatically assuming* that the image is there.

When you eventually stop looking at the sun, it takes your photoreceptors—the cells in our eyes that help us sense light—a couple of minutes to return to normal. During this recovery time, the photoreceptors go through a strange adaptation process, first flashing a positive, then a negative afterimage, then positive, etc. This psychedelic cycle of images can linger for a few seconds, even minutes. It's weird. Andy Warhol captured the positive afterimage effect in his iconic silkscreens of Marilyn Monroe, Elvis Presley, and Jackie O.

Get High Now

Turn on a bright light. Stare at it for two seconds then close your lids, placing your palms over your eyes. You will experience an intense positive afterimage of the light. As your photoreceptors scramble to process the information, they will flash negative afterimages, and then positive again, ad infinitum. Be sure only to do this once, and for a couple seconds. Don't go blind; don't be a solar psycho.

CHROMATIC ILLUSION 🔊

For the past thirty years psychology professor and audio-explorer Diana Deutsch has been experimenting with sound hallucinations in an attempt to uncover how our brains process audio signals. In her research, Deutsch has demonstrated how people can hear completely different patterns in the same set of repeated sounds. It's like how the Carpenters' four-minute-and-ten-second, painfully slow, wrist-cutting depressing version of "Ticket to Ride" sounds so good to some folks (like us) and like dog poop to others (fools).

Chromatic Illusion incorporates two scales that range over two octaves. One scale goes up while the other goes down, with a single tone switching from ear to ear. When played together, some people hear a high scale and a lower scale moving up and down and meeting in the middle every few seconds. Others don't hear scales at all, but random bleeps and bloops. It all depends on how your brain is wired, and how it wants to interpret the tones. Chromatic Illusion becomes even more confusing and fascinating when, after listening to the tracks together, the stereo tracks are played back individually to each ear.

Get High Now

Get a set of headphones and go to Gethighnow.com. Play the Chromatic Illusion audio clip. Listen closely to patterns. Once you've listened with both ears for thirty seconds, press STOP. Now remove the headphones from one ear and just listen to the pattern in the other. Do the same for the other side. Listen to them together. Whoa. Whoa!

Fun Fact: *Psychoacoustics is the study of the psychological and neurological human perception of sound. As food nourishes our physical bodies, sound nourishes our nervous system. Newborns eat food to grow and nurture their cells but they listen to the world around them to feed their neocortex, the part of the brain that controls the "human" functions of conscious thought, perception, language, and more. When sound enters the ear, the frequency—a wave of vibrations—is processed by the brain as electrical pulses. These pulses are transmitted to the brain and processed, giving us "perception." The more sound, the more training the neocortex gets, the more adept and developed it becomes at understanding and contextualizing the world around it. The smarter it/we/you become. That music? Turn it up.*

SCHIZOPHRENIC BLOOD

What do you get when you take the flesh of a freshly hanged man, beat it into a powder, mix with water, then squirt it up your nose? A cure-all for sickness and injuries. Or so thought sixteenth-century European doctors. Other cultures have also used human body parts in attempts to heal ailments. Haitian witch doctors used human skulls as part of classic zombie-making recipes. Seventeenth-century alchemist John Hartman mentions using the pounded brain of a dead young man as a healthful elixir. Which bring us to the point: If so many plants and herbs and even animals (see Giraffe Liver, page 60) get us so high, why can't we get high on *ourselves*?

Dimethyltryptamine, or DMT, is a psychedelic compound that occurs in a plethora of hallucinogenic plants and is also pro-duced in small amounts in the human body. Mentally stable people produce such small amounts of DMT that the effects are unnoticeable. Schizophrenics, however, have been shown in scientific studies to have significantly escalated levels of DMT in their bloodstreams. Is it enough to get high? Terry Southern thought so. The writer penned a short story, "The Blood of a Wig," about a man who seeks to consume a schizophrenic's blood in order to reach a new, top high. Unfortunately (actually, *fortunately*) Southern did not note his sources.

Get High Now

Southern's story is collected in the book *Red Dirt Marijuana & Other Tastes.*

CHROMOTHERAPY

This therapy posits that different colors can evoke physiological changes in our bodies and minds; all we need to do is look at them, feel them, soak them into us. Its practice dates back to ancient Egypt, where the infirmed would be put into rooms illuminated by a specifically colored pane of glass. Egyptians believed bathing rooms in different hues could heal diseases. So did Europeans, who until the 1800s used red drapes in sickrooms to leech disease from patients. The ancient Chinese and Indians also practiced chromotherapy. For the Chinese, every organ had its own healing color; the Ayurvedic Indians ascribed colors to chakras. An imbalance in an organ or chakra would lead to sickness and the surest way to cure it was to expose the body to its deficient color.

Here's where things gets weird: It turns out the Egyptians, Chinese, and Ayurveda weren't too far off. Modern science has proven that colors vibrate in particular frequencies. This is how our visual system distinguishes different colors. Scientists have also discovered that each organ in the body *also* vibrates to a specific frequency. These findings suggest the ancient belief that different colors (which vibrate at specific frequencies) could indeed affect or even heal specific organs (by influencing the organs' specific frequencies) in the same way modern ultrasound surgery works (which vibrates areas of the body with frequencies)! Holy shit!

You're skeptical. We understand. But consider the groundbreaking 1979 "Baker-Miller" report completed by Dr. Alexander Schauss, director of the American Institute for Biosocial Research in Tacoma, Washington. In it, Schauss showed that the shade of "Baker-Miller Pink" painted on prison walls had an extremely tranquilizing effect on its inmates. What's really odd is that Baker-Miller Pink was equally affecting those prisoners who were color-blind, suggesting that the color was influencing something more than the prisoners' ocular senses. The organs, perhaps? The chakras? The astral-goddamn-body?

Get High Now

Consult the Color Affiliations chart below. Paint it violet, indigo, blue, green, yellow, orange, red, aqua, or magenta. Or, easier, just put on some Color Therapy Glasses (see next page).

CHROMOTHERAPY COLOR AFFILIATIONS

Violet: Relaxation; spiritual growth
Indigo: Curing eye, ear, and nasal problems; clear thinking
Blue: Creative expression; clear communication
Green: Rejuvenation
Yellow: Builds nerves; helps depression
Orange: Releases unwanted habits; stimulates thoughts
Red: Remedies female disorders; strength
Aqua: Love and communication; aids grief
Magenta: Balance and vitality

Violet

Indigo

Blue

Green

Yellow

Orange

Red

COLOR THERAPY GLASSES

These "natural healing" glasses are scientifically proven to bring spiritual joy and ecstatic holistic healing into every day of your beautiful life! Actually, no. But they are a great way to cop an illusionary buzz.

Colors that enter our eyes are directed to the hypothalamus, the area in our brains that regulates the nervous system, to the endocrine system via the pituitary gland. This we know. Holistic types argue that when our eyes process a color, the frequency (which is a vibration, and, again, is how we see colors) influences the hypothalamus, which then sends signals to the pituitary. The pituitary sends good-feeling hormones throughout our brain and body. Some holistics argue different colors (different frequencies) can evoke a physiological change in our body. They can hurt us or heal us, changing not only our psychological state but our *physical* state as well. They can get us high. And all this medicinal magic can be done with some really goofy-looking glasses.

Get High Now

A number of color therapy glasses are available online. Usually constructed in a single hue of colored plastic, some color therapy glasses have a New Wave retro-coolness to them. Manufacturers suggest you wear a specific color (from which there are usually a dozen to choose) for about fifteen to thirty minutes a day depending on what you want to affect within your brain and body. High-Lab suggests wearing them *all* day, if not to "synchronize your pituitary gland" then at least to look like that guitarist from Flock of Seagulls.

Note that looking through colored glass—or any other colored film—works just as well, but holding these in front of your eyes for a half hour feels like more trouble than it is worth. Splurge for the shades.

DEPERSONALIZATION

You're in traffic. You're late. The phone rings. You scramble to pick it up. Bump. You've just hit the car in front of you. The phone keeps ringing. You open your door. Coffee spills all over your shirt. Your phone rings. The driver is yelling. You're yelling. *You're late.* And you feel like you're watching yourself in some terrible French movie.

You may not have experienced this particular situation, but you know the feeling: the panic, the high anxiety, the light-headedness, the vertigo, the *depersonalization*—a condition described as being outside of yourself, of watching yourself act in a kind of play, where nothing is real and you no longer control your mental or physical processes. Most common in neurological diseases such as Alzheimer's, Lyme disease, and multiple sclerosis, depersonalization can affect those with clinical depression and other mental ailments. It can also occur when otherwise healthy people suddenly are thrust into very stressful situations.

It's most certainly a high, a potent one. But as much as HighLab loves depersonalization, we don't condone rubbing Lyme-infected ticks on your body in the hopes to get it. What we do condone are recreational panic attacks and self-induced stress fests.

Get High Now

Provoking bouts of panic or stress is tricky. Though HighLab attempted repeatedly to put members in one such situation to experience depersonalization, every participant claimed the process "sucked too much" to continue.

We did however find one self-induced panic exercise that successfully brought on a striking depersonalization high. Here it is: Propose to your publisher a book called *Get High Now!* and set a totally unrealistic deadline to complete it. Stay up night after night with one hand on a pint glass filled with lukewarm green tea, the other on a wireless keyboard that keeps cutting out, trying somehow to be funny. Before you know it, you'll be *out of your fucking mind.*

Chapter Two:

MEDITATIVE HIGHS

YUCATECAN TRANCE INDUCTION BEATS ☺ 👂

In the late 1960s, anthropologist Dr. Felicitas Goodman was hired by the U.S. National Institute of Mental Health to help investigate the religious trance states of 486 societies around the world. Her most revelatory findings weren't in the drug-induced voodoo séances of Haiti or weeks-long meditation ceremonies of Tibet, but in "conservative" Catholic churches throughout the Yucatan of southern Mexico. There, indigenous people had hybridized pagan beliefs with those of Christianity to create a weekly mass service unlike any other.

Part of the mass included Trance Induction Beats, in which a drummer would tap out a pulsing rhythm at 210 beats per minute on a hollow gourd for about a half hour. (Similar tempos were later discovered to induce the deeply relaxing Theta waves in the brain. See page 25.) Goodman discovered this simple technique was effective in lulling not a few, but all members of the church congregation into a deep trance, usually within the first ten minutes.

Wondering if the indigenous Yucatecs were just easily coaxed by Trance Induction Beats, Goodman tested the rhythm on a group of western students, many of whom were not prone to entering trances through other methods. Within fifteen minutes of Yucatecan Trance Induction Beats, every one of the students entered a hypnotic, trance-like state that lasted until the experiment was over.

Get High Now

Yucatecan Trance Induction Beats follow a simple procedure, but, like most induction exercises, each participant must *want* to go there. You've got to believe, star-children.

Either set up your computer's audio to go through your stereo or grab some headphones. Go to Gethighnow.com. Lie on the floor or sit in a chair, wherever you're most comfortable. Doing some preliminary breathing exercises will help get your mind and body in the mood (see Qigong Diaphragmatic Breath, page 230, or Sudarshan Kriya, page 63). When you feel relaxed, start the track. While listening, focus your thoughts on the beating gourd. Relax. Concentrate on the rhythm. Go.

Most people experience dissociation within a few minutes; a deepening of the trance occurs a few minutes later. The track lasts twenty minutes. After that, the path is yours. . . .

Fun Fact: *Goodman found that behaviors classified as "psychotic" in the western world—talking to spirits, seeing dream visions, hearing voices—were perceived as completely normal in a staggering 96 percent of the 486 societies she studied. Those people who* couldn't *access the spirit world were—and still are—considered outcasts in the majority of these societies.*

CHEESE

In 2005, the British Cheese Board enlisted 200 volunteers (100 men, 100 women) in a week-long study to test the old myth that eating cheese before bed caused nightmares. The results were striking: 72 percent of participants slept very well after consuming cheese before bed; 67 percent remembered their dreams, most of which were totally, staggeringly psychedelic. No nightmares were reported by any participants during the course of the study.

The British Dairy Council theorized that the positive sleep experiences were due in part to the large amount of tryptophan in certain cheeses, an amino acid that can reduce stress and induce drowsiness. What's totally unexplained, however, is that eating different cheeses provoked specific types of dreams in the majority of test volunteers, ranging from menial work-related fantasies to truly freakish visions.

Stilton Cheese

This super-fatty blue cheese induced positive sleep experiences five out of seven nights for two-thirds of all participants. Nearly 75 percent of men and 85 percent of women reported vivid, outlandish dreams—some of the most truly fantastical of all cheeses in the study. One subject reported dreaming of a group of soldiers fighting each other with kittens, another dreamed of a series of lifts that moved sidewalks, and one female participant dreamed of a vegetarian crocodile that was sad because it could not eat children.

Cheddar Cheese

This old classic induced dreams related to celebrities in 65 percent of test volunteers. One participant dreamt of being in a football (a.k.a. soccer) match with "Ashley" from *Coronation Street* and the cast of *Emmerdale*—whoever the hell they are.

Cheshire

Dating back to the eleventh century, Cheshire is one of the oldest British cheeses. Yawn. Sorry we were nodding off there. That's because we ate a chunk of Cheshire a half hour ago and are preparing for a boring night of dreamless sleep, which is what 50 percent of participants experienced in the study.

Red Leicester

The crumbly, cheddarish cheese induced "good" sleep experiences with 83 percent of participants. Most common were nostalgic dreams (60 percent), which included visits to childhood homes, revisiting school days, and hanging out with old friends.

Hey, didn't the Kinks record an album about all that? Or was it The Jam? Or The Who? Ah . . . it's so British, isn't it all?

Lancashire

This goopy, stinky cheese gets the HighLab seal of disapproval. Two-thirds of participants under the influence of Lancashire dreamt about work, which, to HighLab should be classified under the label of "nightmare." One of the participants saw herself as the Prime Minister (lame), who engaged in tasks of teaching schools how to choose the best mortgage (lame!). We told you. Nightmare.

Get High Now

All participants in the British Dairy Council study ate 20 grams (0.7 ounces) of a particular cheese a half hour before normal sleep time every night for one week. Saunter on down to your local cheese shop, pick up a half pound of a cheese of your choice (soon to be known on the streets as *magic mold*) and prepare yourself for a brain-melting night's rest.

RINZAI ZEN COSMIC EGG

The Rinzai Zen sect was introduced to Japan in 1191 and today boasts over two million followers. Unlike other Buddhist sects, Rinzai Zenists go through often exhaustive and rigorous exercises in their pursuit of *kensho*—seeing one's true nature. The Cosmic Egg hand position is not one of these strenuous exercises. It is simple, easy, and pain-free. HighLab found it calming and centering, and it helped us focus on larger life issues outside the fact that the floor on which we were all sitting was completely covered in dog fur, spilled catnip tea, and weeks-old Post-It note reminders to sweep and mop the floor before attempting another Cosmic Egg session.

Get High Now

Sit comfortably in a chair or on the floor. Place your hands in your lap, just above your navel. Open your right palm and rest your left palm within it, with your thumbs barely touching each other, but not

pressed together. Relax your shoulders, breathe deeply and completely. Remember that the figure your hand position is mimicking is not just any egg, it's a Cosmic Egg—a receiver and keeper of the energies and wisdom of the universe.

RUSSIAN SLEEP

Also known as the electrosleep machine, the Russian Sleep device was developed (indeed) in Russia in the 1960s to cut down by one-eighth the amount of time soldiers needed to rest per night to feel refreshed. It worked like this: A "volunteer" would sit in a chair with one electrode adhered behind the ear and another on top of the eyelid. The machine would then deliver repeated one-millisecond shocks of 100 Hz to each electrode. The Soviets asserted that a single thirty-minute session on a Russian Sleep machine was equivalent to about eight hours of sleep. The soldiers believed it (well, they had no choice), and worked "consciously" for days while wasting almost no time for rest.

Years later, the U.S. military created its own electrosleep machines and used them in attempts to cure insomnia, anxiety, and depression. Results were very poor at best, not to mention one bitter side effect: Within a few days of nothing but Russian Sleep, most subjects would begin experiencing vivid dreams during waking hours. Oops.

Get High Now

Log on to eBay. Buy Russian Sleep machine. Work twenty-three-and-a-half-hour days. Dream during waking hours. Eat borscht. Want to die.

WOW!
HERMANN'S SPARKLING GRID!

When overfed, the stomach regurgitates *Joseph and His Technicolor Dreamcoat*. The same thing happens when we overfeed the brain (see Sensory Overload, page 71), but instead of vomit the brain hurls hallucinations, distorted perceptions, and other coolness. We like that. Which is why we like *Wow! Hermann's Sparkling Grid!* This illusionary high was created in 1870 by German speech researcher Ludimar Hermann (1838–1914). The most popular (and controversial) theory is that the illusion works by

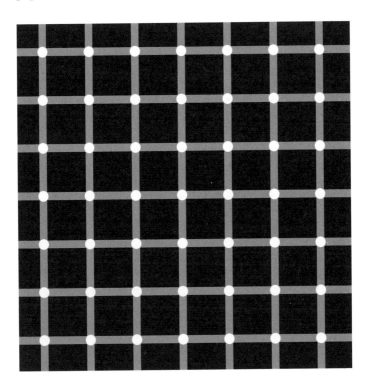

stimulating the neurons in our eyes so much that they shut off the neurons near them in a process known as *lateral inhibition.*

Here is how it works: When photoreceptors—the neurons in our eyes that detect areas of light—focus on the *center* of Hermann's grid, they detect increased brightness. The photoreceptors turn on the visual system's ganglion cells, which send the "brightness" information to the brain. However, details from the *peripheral* areas of Hermann's grid confuse the eyes. There are too many lines, squares, and dots to process. The photoreceptors react by turning off some of the ganglion cells in these peripheral areas. The brain, confused by these counteracting on/off signals, reacts by stabilizing the areas of center focus, and flashes the areas in the peripheral vision as it processes them on then off, on then off. As you concentrate on different areas of the grid, the flashing areas shift.

Get High Now

Look at it! Look at it! Look at it!

⚠ WARNING: The above is an unproven, simplified, and semi-hybridized theory compounded for you by two people: me and the really tired guy staring at me in the reflection of the computer monitor. If you are annoyed by the brevity of this explanation we invite you to apply for a neuroscience degree at your favorite university . . . or better, *f*#! off*! Now, can we get *high* already?

INVERSION TABLE SENSORY-DEPRIVATION HALLUCINATIONS

Inversion therapies—various forms of hanging upside down—have been used for over two thousand years. Around 400 B.C., Hippocrates strung up patients with rope and pulleys in an attempt to cure headaches and back pain. In the late 1980s

MacGyver used inversion to keep himself looking great in his hot television show.

Today, proponents of inversion boast that the exercise increases flexibility, releases tension in the spine, relieves stress, and more. Many orthopedic surgeons contest these claims, saying inversion is unlikely to help anything and may even be harmful, possibly *provoking* headaches and increased hypertension. But one thing everyone agrees on is that inversion gets you high. This is caused, according to some, by the increase in blood flow to the brain and heart induced by hanging upside down. More blood flow means more oxygen to the brain, which produces a clear-headed, slightly spaceyish high. Rosie O'Donnell used inversion to overcome depression. *The Da Vinci Code* author Dan Brown used it to overcome writer's block. HighLab uses it to hallucinate.

To maximize the psychedelic and hallucinatory effects, High-Lab incorporated sensory-deprivation techniques into a standard

inversion exercise. Within twenty minutes of using this technique, members experienced some mildly colorful visual field alterations, full body tingling, and a high that lasted for a few hours. Best of all, it made our backs feel *so good*. HighLab believes this is why all those orthopedic surgeons naysay inversion—if everyone inverted, those suckers would be out of work.

Get High Now

Grocery List:

- Inversion table
- Ear plugs
- Blindfold

Set the inversion table up in a quiet room. Put in your earplugs and place blindfold on the forehead, just above your eyes. Make sure your weight is perfectly centered so that even the slightest alteration on the table affects the angle at which you are lying. Once you are comfortable on the table put the blindfold over your eyes. Forget about time, tasks, daily chores. Feel your body and mind drift off. Turn. Over.

NOTING

While in the preliminary stages of meditation, most of us will experience a constant barrage of random thoughts: We'll obsess over little details of work, remember forgotten appointments, make lists of chores. We'll get antsy. This is natural. Our minds are overburdened with responsibilities, they are conditioned to be constantly *on*—thinking, plotting, acting. It's hard to turn them off.

The exercise of *Noting* first identifies how and when the mind slips, then helps reroute our concentration back to the task at hand. Doing this allows us to sink deeper into meditative exercises, as well as gives context to what is really important in our sad—correction: *amazing and fascinating*—lives.

When Noting, you will be labeling the thought processes in the body into two categories: *thoughts* and *feelings*. For instance, suppose while trying to meditate, you have an itch on your knee. Normally, this itch might make you lose concentration. You may begin asking yourself if you scraped the knee against poison ivy while hiking, if there is an ant crawling on you, etc. The mind drifts.

While Noting, the goal is to simply label the itch: *feeling – itch*. You acknowledge it, note its category (*feeling*) and a general subcategory (*itch*), then return to meditating. The same process is applied to thoughts. When meditating and your concentration slips, note to yourself in general terms what it is you are thinking of. For instance, if you remember you need to take out the garbage, note *thought – task*. Acknowledge the category: *thought*, subcategory: *task*, and move on.

With practice, Noting will help clear your mind and become singly connected in the here and now—an all too rare treat in our stressful, overburdened lives.

Get High Now

Sit comfortably on the floor or in a chair. Close your eyes. Take inventory of the senses in your body. Treat them all objectively, as you would books on a shelf in your room. You may hear a car outside: note *thought – noise*. You may feel the socks on your feet: note *feeling – clothes*. You may be thinking of all the e-mails you need to respond to tonight: note *thought – tasks*. Don't think about the categories or subcategories—name them quickly and return your focus.

Once you get the hang of it, try to strip your Noting subcategories (clothes, tasks, etc.). Everything that enters your mind becomes simply a feeling or a thought. Eventually, and with practice, categories will be unnecessary and so will Noting. That's the whole point of the exercise: to help you one day be able to close your eyes and forget about all your trivialities, thoughts, fears, and give yourself to the moment. Take *note*.

Helpful Hint: Try Noting before you attempt a meditation or breathwork exercise. See how it helps.

DILL

This flowery herb gets its name from *dilla*, which translates from Norse as "to soothe or lull." Dill has been used since as early as 3,000 B.C. Its first medicinal mention comes from an Egyptian medical text claiming it as an effective herb to induce deep relaxation and sleepiness. Ancient Greeks used it to make love potions (i.e., ancient roofies) that would lull (i.e., drug) a loved one (i.e, unsuspecting date) into one's caring arms (i.e., sex chamber).

It gets its power from its high levels of naturally occurring limonene and carvone, both hydrocarbons that induce calmness in the body. Dill oil mixed with water is still today a popular remedy for infant colic. More potent mixtures help adults soothe stomachaches, cramps, and insomnia. Dill is popular in Chinese medicine for chest congestion, skin diseases, and flu symptoms. The oil is an effective antibacterial.

With this proud millennia-long history (and exceptionally detailed research from yours truly) you'd expect the dill high to be amazing, even life-changing. You'd expect wrong. At best the dill high is very mellow, but consider so is *The Best of Bread*, and that album rules.

Get High Now

How much dill you should quaff depends on what you're looking to get out of the good herb. About 6 drops of dill oil in a glass of water with sugar is a popular infusion for calming nerves and stomach ailments. HighLab's nutritionist tells us that steeping 2 to 4 tablespoons of dill seed in a cup of hot water for ten minutes, and then straining and drinking as a tea is a good way to induce a sleepy, rubbery-feeling high. Alternately, you can throw about 3 grams of dill seed into a soup or salad for slightly stronger effects. Or, you could just start slamming pickles; however, by the time you copped a dill buzz you'll most certainly be hurling relish.

TRANSCENDENTAL MEDITATION (A Primer)

Practiced by over six million people, Transcendental Meditation (TM) is a simple meditation technique developed by Maharishi Mahesh Yogi that involves repeating a simple phrase, or mantra, for twenty minutes once or twice a day. Studies by *Science, Scientific American*, and others showed significant physiological changes within those who practiced TM meditation, including reduced cholesterol, decreased blood pressure, stronger immune system health, increased brain function, and numerous other benefits. But what's attracted many rockers and starlets to TM for the past fifty years are the consciousness-expanding psychological effects of the practice.

The Doors met at a TM seminar. The Beatles went to India in 1968 to learn TM in-person from Maharishi Mahesh Yogi. (They left after Maharishi allegedly tried to grope Mia Farrow and numerous other groupies. Which brings us to another benefit of TM: it purportedly increases the sex drive.) Today, David Lynch, Howard Stern, and many other rich-and-famous attribute at least part of their success and creativity to a daily TM practice.

TM Gurus claim, after extended practice, subjects would have "the ability to perceive things which are beyond the reach of the senses, the development of profound intimacy and support from one's physical environment, and even such abilities as disappearing and rising up or levitating at will." Fun! HighLab did not experience such radness in our trials with TM, but after about a week of daily meditation we did experience a full mental and body high that lingered throughout the day. The longer and more we practiced TM, the better we felt. Best of all, the exercise is so easy.

Note: Below is a simple TM exercise HighLab freestyled off some-one who had attended TM seminars. Though the more profound benefits of TM are usually only received after numerous sessions, one-off exercise offers a quick and fulfilling soul-buzz. As with many other meditation highs in this book, we encourage anyone curious about TM to investigate the practice under the guidance of a seasoned teacher.

Get High Now

Pick a mantra (see below). Sit comfortably on the floor or in a chair. Inhale slowly through your nose, then hold that breath for a count of *two* before exhaling. Close your eyes. Repeat this about five times or until you feel fully relaxed with this rhythm. When ready, take a deeper breath and softly chant your mantra aloud as you exhale. Speak it clearly, feeling the vibrations of each phrase fill your body and mind. The pace of your exhales and the mantra will soon join in a natural way after a few repetitions. Don't worry about breathing too quickly or slowly or uncluttering your mind of thoughts—just relax and follow the rhythm of the mantra. Just *be* . . .

After ten minutes or so, stop chanting and *internalize* your mantra: Listen to it ring throughout your body. Switch back to verbalizing it whenever you feel comfortable. There is no right or wrong way—any method that works for you is the right method. HighLab suggests ten minutes of verbal chanting, ten minutes of internal chanting. When you are done, inhale one last deep breath and open your eyes. You just underwent a physiological change. Your mind, body, and soul are now perfectly tuned. It feels so right.

Choosing a Mantra

Translated from Sanskrit as "to free from the mind," mantras are phrases or poems chanted in Hindu, Buddhist, Sikh, and numerous other meditation exercises.

When we vocalize a phrase, we produce a physical vibration within us that we later associate with feelings or meanings (see Toning, page 105). It's the *feeling* of the phrase we learn to understand. This is the premise upon which many mantras are based—it's how they *feel* that's important; their meaning is secondary.

According to yogis, prolonged mantra chanting will eventually drown out all other thoughts, sensations, and ailments in the body. Soon you will hear only the mantra, think only the mantra while meditating. You will become the mantra. This sounds brainwashingly scary, but it is a good thing. Mantra meditations relax the body and mind; they let us forget about the trivialities in day-to-day life and focus on the universe at large. Mantras get us cosmically high.

Get High Now

Below are some common Buddhist mantras. Try them with TM, Samatha Level Dhammakāya Meditation (page 242), and Kundalini Transcendent Chanting (page 36).

om swasti jampal yang sog kun gye pai lam
(You radiate as manifestations of profound and vast dharma.)

oh ah hum vajra guru padma siddhi hum
(I invoke you, the Vajra Guru, Padmasambhava; by your blessing, may you grant us supreme blessings.)

om mani padme hum
(Can't really be translated: invokes compassion through Chenrezig, the Tibetan embodiment of compassion. The two middle words mean "the jewel in the lotus.")

om namah shivaya
(The "great redeeming" mantra. Translates roughly to "bow to Shiva." In Hindu mythology Shiva symbolizes, among other things, the inner self, which remains intact even after everything in the world is gone.)

HighLab's favorite!
gatay, gatay, paragatay, parasamgatay, bodhi svaha
(From the *Heart Sutra*: Gone, Gone, Gone Beyond, Gone Completely Beyond, So Be Awakened!)

LUCID DREAM INDUCTIONS

The popularity of lucid dreaming has grown rapidly in recent years, wending its way into movies, books, and Santa Barbara–weekend workshops. But unlike other quasi-mystical trends Hollywood starlets have glommed onto like indigo children and leg warmers, lucid dreaming is not lame. It actually works.

A lucid dream is one in which you know you are sleeping. Most people enter these unexpectedly, and when they do are often confused or frightened by the experience. Lucid Dream Inductions allow you to control not only when and how you enter a lucid dream, but what to do once you get there. Later, inductions can teach you how to use dreams to fulfill ambitions in waking life. Or just get high. HighLab members who mastered the initial Lucid Dream Inductions reported having some of the most vivid, visceral, and mind-blowingly weird dream experiences of their lives. Some were frightening; others empowering.

Mnemonic Induction of Lucid Dreams (MILD)

Get High Now

While lying in bed before sleep, concentrate single-mindedly on your intention to have a lucid dream. Imagine yourself in some sort of fantastic scenario—moonwalking on, say, the moon. Tell yourself repeatedly that you will have a lucid dream about the subject, *about moonwalking on the moon.* When your thoughts stray, bring them back to lucid dreaming. Let yourself drift off, feel your body falling asleep, but keep the thought in your head: *moonwalk on the moon, moonwalk on the moon, moonwalk on the moon.* . . . While the training methods to induce lucid dreams may be simple, successfully entering and staying in a lucid dream can be difficult, and takes practice. Stick with it: Most people see results after about a week.

Dream Recall Method for Induction of Lucid Dreams (DRMILD)

Get High Now

Before going to sleep, reimagine a dream you recently had. Recall where you were, what you were doing, and in what environment the dream took place. Now place yourself within the dream, become a character in it, stroll around, interact with your surroundings. Be the focal point of the dream and repeatedly remind yourself that you are in it. The goal here is to ensure that the last thing on your mind before falling asleep is your *intention* to be in a lucid dream.

> **Fun Fact:** *Once in a lucid dream, try rubbing your hands. In a test group of 34 volunteers led by psychophysiologist Stephen LaBerge, this simple action showed a 90 percent success rate in prolonging lucid dreams.*

Wake-Back-to-Bed Lucid Dream Induction (WBTB)

Researcher Stephen LaBerge claims a 60 percent success rate for Lucid Dream Induction with Wake-Back-to-Bed methods. It works by manipulating your REM sleep cycle—the cycle in which lucid dreams occur—which most people enter after five hours of rest. By waking in the middle of this cycle, you will be putting your brain on pause; when you finally go back to sleep, the brain is geared to immediately return to REM sleep. This makes hopping into lucid dreams easier and enables longer and more memorable experiences. Two members of HighLab who experimented with WBTB successfully entered a lucid dream in their first attempt.

Get High Now

Spend a day vigorously exercising or doing some task that will ensure you are tired at the end of the day. Before bed, take note of the time and set your alarm clock for five hours later.

When the alarm wakes you up, get out of bed. Read or stay busy for an hour. When you are set to return to sleep, follow the mnemonic induction technique, page 99.

Helpful Hint: One technique to help stay in a lucid dream is "spinning." While in the lucid dream, simply try to spin your body in circles. This action will provoke your mind to remain in REM sleep a bit longer, allowing the dream to continue. In a study conducted by Stephen LaBerge, spinning showed a staggering 90 percent success rate in prolonging lucid dreams.

Wake-Initiation of Lucid Dreams (WILD)

This powerful, sometimes frightening Lucid Dream Induction method occurs when the sleeper enters REM sleep directly from a waking state. It's easiest to practice WILD in the middle of regular nightly rest or during a nap.

Using the WILD method, HighLab members experienced psychedelic, sometimes violent inductions into the lucid dream state, which included initial dizziness, twirling, extremely loud audio hallucinations, and other weird shit. The lucid dreams experienced after this initial state of confusion were some of the more powerful and truly baffling HighLab members could recall. Beware.

Get High Now

Note: These steps are similar to Wake-Back-to-Bed Lucid Dream Induction (see facing page) but offer very different outcomes.

Step One: Set your alarm five hours in advance of the time you are preparing to go to sleep. What you will be doing is waking yourself in what is the usual REM cycle of sleep. As you fall back asleep your mind will be conditioned to enter directly back into REM, the cycle in which lucid dreams occur, sending you from the waking state to the lucid state in what appears to be an instant.

Step Two: Once the alarm goes off, try to fall back to sleep as you normally would, but this time imagine walking slowly down a spiral staircase. Imagine the light fading a bit with each step. As you continue down, stay conscious that you are *thinking* about walking down the staircase. The mind will slip into random thoughts. Bring it back. Remember that you are telling yourself to walk down the stairs, each stair. You are in control. Do not let your mind slip. Then . . . slip.

FISH HEADS

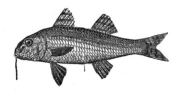

In 2006, two British men sat down in their favorite restaurant and ordered *Sarpa salpa*, a fish common in the eastern Atlantic and Mediterranean. An hour after eating the fish, one man began experiencing "terrifying visual and auditory hallucinations"; the other (who was ninety years old!) soon joined in the madness. Both experienced intense waking dream visions for 36 solid hours while recovering in the hospital. Vivid nightmares persisted for two nights after. Yikes.

According to Luc De Haro and Philip Pommier, two doctors who took up the case at Centre Antipoison, Hôpital Salvator, Marseille, France, the Britons had both experienced *ichthyoallyeinotoxism*. This rare food poisoning occurs after eating the heads or body parts of certain fish that have ingested algae or plankton containing *indole*, an organic compound that in certain stages of development can share the same tryptophan-derived tryptamine alkaloids (a.k.a. *stuff*) as the hallucinogens LSD and DMT.

Et tu, Rabbitfish? It's not just the Sarpa salpa that can carry ichthyoallyeinotoxism: mullet, tangs, goatfish, and rabbitfish can all be hallucinogenic. In fact, three thousand years ago ichthyoallyeinotoxism was so common Romans harvested certain Mediterranean fish with the "sole" intent of getting high. Some historians say these dream fish inspired the ancients to come up with some of the insanely creepy Roman mythology. *Auxilio ab alto!*

Get High Now

Skip the salad, Caesar. Go straight to the fillet of goatfish.

TROXLER'S FADING ◉

This visual high was created in 1804 by Swiss physician, philosopher, and friend of Beethoven, Ignaz Paul Vital Troxler. It works by taking advantage of the lazy neurons in our vision system. Within about thirty seconds of staring at Troxler's Fading, the neurons controlling our peripheral vision get bored and concentrate their energy on the center of the image. Our brains begin to tunnel our visual field and eventually remove details from the periphery around the spot in which we are concentrating. This hallucination is enhanced if the image is small and blurred, as it is in most Troxler's Fading examples.

Get High Now

Go to Gethighnow.com. Stare at the ◉ in the middle of the image. You will first see the rotating dot changing color. Soon, whoa, the surrounding dots just disappear, like so many Lays Potato Chips left near a handsome couple picnicking in the park.

EXTENDED CANDLE OBSERVATION

The brain hates to be lazy. All it wants is attention—constant input. Deny it sound for long enough, and, baby-like, it will throw a tantrum of imaginary words and noises in our heads (see Inversion Table Sensory Deprivation Hallucinations, page 91,

and Wow! Hermann's Sparkling Grid!, page 90). Deny it visual stimulation and it will do the same, regurgitating a kaleidoscope of colors and patterns and other errata into our vision.

Some consider the lazy-brain hallucinations distracting, while others find them disarming and frightening. For those of us who like to get high without drugs, however, we consider them as blessings from sweet, sweet Jesus. They are easy. All you need is a candle, a dark room, and a few minutes.

Get High Now

Bring a candle and matches into a dark room. Set an alarm to go off in seven minutes. Place the candle a few feet from your face on a coffee table, desk, whatever. Light the candle and stare at the flame. Stare at it. Try not to blink. If you find your mind wandering, ask yourself just to stay perfectly quiet, unmoving, for ten more seconds. When those ten seconds are up, ask yourself to spend just ten seconds more. Keep staring. Keep searching. Concentrate. Your field of vision will eventually widen. Within a couple minutes, your brain will grow bored and start infusing your field of vision with random colors and images. Yes, really. It seems too simple to actually work . . . until you try it. Now go observe the candle, enter the flame.

TONING ☺

When we speak to others, we are also speaking within ourselves. Each word that projects from us also sends vibrations throughout our mouths and our bodies. As such, we internalize our spoken expressions, forming our understanding not only by the way words sound but how they *feel*. The practice of stimulating or calming our minds and bodies by meditating on spoken words is called Toning. (Yes, that last paragraph reads like a copy block yanked from a hack holistic therapist's MySpace page, but the premise of Toning is based on science, not hashish. Now read on.)

For the past thirty years, Toning has grown exponentially and is now endorsed by everyone from medical doctors to teachers to corporate folks. What attracts them is the clearheaded, calming feeling they get while practicing Toning exercises, as well as the lingering benefits, which can include enhanced speaking ability, more acute concentration, and sharper listening power. These benefits, Toners claim, are a result of the voice-ear connection you create when simultaneously speaking and thinking words. Connecting the voice with the ear allows the brain to better correlate reactions, senses, and mental functions—not to mention the meditative high it offers after just a couple rounds.

Get High Now

The same way different yoga poses stretch different muscle groups, different tones stimulate different parts of the mind and body. Some awaken you; others relax. Try some. *Tone* some.

Morning Toning: Sit comfortably in a chair or on the floor. Close your eyes if you'd like. Now breathe in through your nose slowly to a count of about *five*. Exhale at the same speed. Do this three times.

After the fourth inhale, slowly speak aloud the tone group *UU-AH-EE-MM* as you exhale. Relax your throat. Close your lips about halfway through the *MM* sound, feel it reverberate in your mouth, let it fill your body. Each exhaled tone group should last about ten seconds, with the final *MM* lingering until you are out of breath. Repeat for at least three minutes.

Next, speak the entire tone group with your mouth closed, inhaling and exhaling as you did before. Accentuate each vowel, feeling the tones in your nasal cavity. As you repeat the phrase, place your hands around your body—the chest, back, neck. Feel how each vowel resonates in different parts throughout your body. The *UU-AH-EE-MM* tone group is used to balance the energy throughout the mind and body. Repeat it for a minimum of three minutes. Keep going and stop when you like. There is no right and wrong way to get *Tone Loc'd*.

Bonus High

Night Toning: Follow the steps for **Morning Toning** but tone the group *"MM-EE-AH-UU."* This will bring you balance and relaxation before a night of rest.

VOWEL	STIMULATES
UU ("who")	lower spine, for relaxation and centeredness.
OH ("go")	center of the chest, for concentration.
AH ("car")	heart, for emotions.
EY ("pray")	throat area, for communication.
EE ("knee")	head, for creative energy.
MM (humming, lips closed)	mouth and tongue, for balance.

KAVA

Named for both the plant and the ubiquitous drink from which it is made, kava is an indelible part of traditional South Pacific culture from Hawaii to Papua New Guinea, and has been celebrated for over three thousand years as a natural cure-all and community elixir.

The drink is made by mashing the fresh or dried roots of the kava plant, adding water, straining, then serving the kava tea in a coconut half-shell. It is traditionally imbibed at sundown as part of nightly village gatherings. One to two cups produces a numbing sensation in the mouth and tongue followed by a clear-headedness and a soft, tranquilized feeling. Three or more cups produce mild perception hallucinations and euphoria. Four or more cups transform the body into a semi-conscious primordial soup—a soft, wet, human pillow, which can be good or bad depending on your preferences.

Kava is legal throughout the United States and most other countries, classified under the same umbrella of foods as coffee and tea. As of January 2009, it is still illegal in Switzerland, France, and the Netherlands. Kava is most popularly ingested in pill form as a supplement. HighLab does not condone taking concentrated amounts of kava in pill form or any artificial state. Germany banned kava in 2002, stating excessive use over time could adversely affect the liver. (They have since lifted this ban, stating the evidence that kava was unsafe was in error.) Either way, what all this means: Polynesians and Melanesians have been drinking kava in its natural state for millennia and enjoyed generally fantastic health, with few if any recorded liver ailments caused by the good root. Stick with the old ways.

Get High Now

In the past, a male virgin member of the village (chosen for his "purity") would masticate and spit the kava root into a community bowl from which cupfuls were drunk. This process produces a more potent kava, as the enzyme in human saliva breaks down more of the *kavalactones*, the psychoactive ingredient in the plant. But drinking another's spit, beyond being repulsive, can also lead to the spread of diseases like tuberculosis. Most islanders have turned to preparing dried kava, in which they put about a cup of pounded root in some pantyhose or cheesecloth, and strain about four pints of water through it. Then drink. Then (don't) think.

HIGHLAB: GETTING RESULTS

As part of our semi-scientific research, one member of HighLab spent two weeks on the island of Tanna in the South Pacific nation of Vanuatu in the fall of 2001, living with yam farmers and drinking kava every night with the village chief—an 82-year-old man who attributed his seventy years of perfect health, perfect teeth, and razor-sharp mental acumen to his nightly kava drinking. The High-Lab member drank the kava in the "traditional ways" freshly masticated by a male "virgin." He found the effects of the good kava root to be chakra-shakingly intense—his bones become bungee cords, his mind transformed into the ever-seeing eye of Qat, the

Ni-Vanuatu god who created the Vanuatu islands and covered them with plant and animal life. The member looks forward to his next trip back to the "Big Blue."

TIBETAN BUDDHIST LIGHT MEDITATION

This exercise, though it's going to sound New Age-y, has been central to Tibetan Buddhist meditation for thousands of years for a reason: It works. It requires a shirking of your cloak of irony, and your sincere intention and concentrated visualization. If you don't feel ready to give that, move on to Moth Larva (page 49); if you feel ready, go forth, Grasshopper. All members of HighLab found this to be an earnestly revitalizing and comforting exercise. Light up.

Get High Now

Step One: Lie down somewhere comfortable. Close your eyes. Envision your body and mind as being filled with total, deep blackness. Now imagine a cold and sad place. This place, this cold feeling in your body, is weighing you down. You feel alone. Dwell here for a few minutes. Sink deeper. Feel the cold.

Step Two: Imagine within this blackness the tiniest speck of light— a distant and twinkling star. Find it and study it. This light is in you, coming from you. Watch this tiny light grow slowly larger within you. It is cutting through the darkness. Focus on it. Watch it grow. Look at what's around it. See how it is very bright, filling your body with white light. Let it sit there within you. Hold this thought for a minute. Soon the light is penetrating every cell of your body, filling you completely as it grows larger, brighter, and warmer. It now fills every fiber of your being. Where there was once stress and worry, there is now only light, complete and full bright white light. Open your eyes.

CARAWAY

Caraway seeds aren't seeds at all but the fruit of a flowering green shrub, one of the oldest cultivated spices in history. Julius Caesar prized caraway for its restorative qualities, feeding soldiers loads of it in his specially baked Roman meal bread. The ancient Greeks used caraway oil to imbue a glowing appearance in the skin. Medieval folk cherished it for its spiritual powers, claiming a pocket of caraway would protect a wearer from having property stolen. Since then, the little seeds—rather fruits—have been used to aid in digestion and stave off intestinal gas. Some still use it as a mild sedative. Some, like you, tonight.

Get High Now

The effects of caraway are very mellow at best, but not unpleasant. One night, bored with Soul Dancing (page 39), two HighLab members feasted on a teaspoonful. The flavor was invigorating, with a touch of mint. About an hour later, a very mild "lotiony" feeling and a kind of clear-headedness took over. Each member claimed the effects were identical to taking an aspirin for a headache, but without having the headache.

SELF-HYPNOTISM

What happens when someone says something that embarrasses you? Compliments you? Flirts with you? Your face may flush red, you might smile. These actions are uncontrollable: You don't realize they are happening to your body until after they have already begun to occur. What has happened is that someone else has used words or movements to trigger a physiological reaction in your body. You got hypnotized.

Hypnotism has been used for centuries in speeches, courting rituals, in church, even in the arts. Rachmaninoff had a therapist hypnotize him to overcome writer's block to finish his masterful and wondrous Piano Concerto No. 2. You can hypnotize yourself to get high.

⚠ WARNING: Some people are very susceptible to hypnosis. For them, these exercises can lead to hours-long trances or longer. As a precaution, set an alarm for fifteen minutes from the time you begin each of these self-hypnosis highs. Seriously—do this.

Get High Now

Coin Induction: Grab a coin and sit in a chair someplace quiet where you won't be disturbed.

To begin, relax one hand on your lap. In the other hand, hold the coin between your thumb and index finger, then extend that arm directly in front of you. Point your fingers downward. Notice your arm, the slight arch of your hand. Look at your skin, how it smoothly stretches over your arm. If you are wearing long sleeves, concentrate on the fabric covering the arm, its creases and texture. Focus on your arm for about three minutes. When your mind drifts, pull it back. Concentrate.

Now, while still holding the coin in front of you, tell yourself that when you are ready to transition, your fingers will relax, your tendons will loosen, muscles will soften, the coin will drop. You will only relax this arm and drop the coin when you are completely ready to enter a trance. Some people are ready for this transition in a matter of seconds, others take minutes. You will know when you are ready. Only then will the coin drop.

As a precaution, the alarm will sound after a few minutes. (If it sounds before you enter the trance, set it ten minutes ahead and repeat the steps again.)

Most people are susceptible to some form of self-hypnosis, while others may not ever be able to induce a trance. How do you know if you can hypnotize yourself? Say you can and try it.

Gluey Hands: Sit comfortably in a chair. Put your hands in your lap, palms up. Stare at your hands. Relax. Look at your fingers. Keep staring. Tell yourself there is glue on your fingers. Focus. Watch as the glue settles, adhering to your skin. Keep staring. Do this for a couple minutes.

When you feel as though the glue has set entirely, try to move your fingers and your hands apart. If you can do this, start again; the glue was not on your skin long enough to adhere. This time imagine

more glue is on your hands; this glue is stronger and will set quicker. Focus. When you feel ready, try to pull your hands apart. You can't. They are stuck together. You are now self-hypnotized.

Fun Fact: *Your susceptibility to being hypnotized is directly related to how much white is visible when you roll your eyes back in your head. The more white, the more easily and deeply you will be able to fall into a hypnotic state.*

NONSEXUAL PUBLIC NUDITY

On a freezing day in winter two members of HighLab went out for some Thalassotherapy (page 206) at a nude beach fifteen miles south of our beloved San Francisco. Neither member had any interest in nudity, rather we liked the beach for its solitude and occasionally challenging surf. As we rappelled down the steep cliff to the beach break, we noticed an elderly man leaning against a piece of driftwood. As a frigid Arctic wind was blowing in from the north he stood there meditating, a smile on his face, a deep sense of solace in his eyes, totally naked.

The high this old man was getting standing nude in public is shared by millions of people around the world every day. Nudists and their "naturist" brethren claim the practice liberates the spirit, offering a full physical, mental, and spiritual high that is as wholesome as it is potent. Naturist and author Marc Alain Descamps and others posit that some of the high from nonsexual public nudity may be biological. Going naked in the day exposes more of the body to sunlight, allowing the body to soak up more Vitamin D. This, some naturists argue, improves mood and can help cure diseases such as tuberculosis and rheumatism.

Get High Now

Take it off.

RESULTANT TONES ⑨

This sonic phenomenon occurs when two notes—one higher than the other—are played simultaneously, resulting in a *phantom* tone that shares a pitch with neither of the two notes being played. What happens is the specific frequencies of the two notes clash in such a way that an additional frequency—either the sum or the difference of these vibrations—is created. Sound researchers refer to *Resultant Tones* as "ghost notes"; HighLab refers to them as a creepy high.

Get High Now

Go to Gethighnow.com and click on Resultant Tones. What you'll be hearing is two flute tones perfectly tuned to the key of A (440 Hz). One flute track will play a C (the twelfth above) as the other will play the E-flat above that C. When flutists play these notes at the same time, an A-flat two octaves higher will be heard—and so will its magical Resultant Tone be heard a third below.

EQUILUMINANCE ◉

Fools teach us not to make assumptions because doing so puts us at risk of being wrong. (Ever hear the corporate saying, "*Assume* makes an *ass* out of *u* and *me*"?) Yet do these fools know that being wrong can be fun? Take for instance our visual system: When it makes wrong assumptions it makes an ass of nobody, it makes us high—giving us a multihued visual diaspora coupled with a disjointed, disoriented feeling.

Equiluminance is a display in which the color components are organized in such a way as to trick our eyes (and brains). What happens is the colors in the image are so close in luminance (brightness) that they are recognized by our color-sensitive perceptions but not our luminance-sensitive perceptions. This discretion makes a stationary object appear as though it were moving.

Old billboards used equiluminance to make objects appear animated, even though they were just flashing sets of stationary lights. The animated link below will show you how it all works.

Get High Now

Go to Gethighnow.com and click Equiluminance.

You will be looking at four sets of images that each flash for a second before the next image appears. The first flashed image is of black-and-white squares; the second image is of green-and-red squares, positioned a half-block off of the black-and-white squares. The third image is, again, black-and-white squares placed a half-block from the previous green-and-red square. The final image is of green-and-red squares, a half-square off the previous block.

As these four block images flash in order one at a time in front of each other, our brains assume the darker colors (red and black) together and the lighter colors (green and white) together. This assumption, which is caused by our ability to distinguish the *color* but not the *luminance* of the image, gives these four stationary images the illusion that they are in perpetual motion, moving forward.

FELDENKRAIS BOOK BALANCING METHOD

Dr. Moshe Feldenkrais (1904–1984), a Ukrainian-born engineer and judo enthusiast, believed the key to good health and mental enlightenment was to become physically flexible. Being flexible, he believed, connects us more closely with natural movements, thoughts, and feelings, and opens us to experiences of self-discovery.

Feldenkrais's instruction included a system called "Awareness Through Movement" (ATM), which consists of over a thousand lessons. He believed that showing us how to move about in comfort can improve our perception of what we *think* and *feel* our bodies are capable of. This not only boosts our self-image but also provides us with an enormous sense of physical and mental well-being.

Get High Now

Step One: Gather four books of similar size and place them in a stack on the floor. (Note: *Get High Now* was specially designed to be the perfect weight and size for this exercise. Please go buy three more copies.)

Step Two: Take your socks off and remove any sweaters, hats, or bulky clothing. Pants and T-shirt are best. Lie on your back on the floor.

Step Three: Lift one leg up so that the sole of your foot is facing the ceiling. Grab a book, lean up, and balance the book on that foot.

Step Four: When you feel the book is stable, place another book on the other foot in the same manner. Become aware of which body parts you are using to hold the books in place.

Step Five: Grab another book and place it in the middle of your opposite open palm, also parallel to the floor. Position it so that it is stable, centered on the hand.

Step Six: Grab the final book and, using your fingers, position it in the center of the palm of the hand that just picked it up.

Step Seven: You should now be balancing all four books, one on each hand and foot. Feel the weight of each book on your appendages. Focus on the amazing web of muscles and tendons you are employing to hold up these books. Move the books up and down on each limb, feel the changes in your body. Close your eyes. Center yourself.

Bonus High for Advanced Trippers

Once balancing all four books, roll your body so that your stomach faces the floor, then keep rolling until you are again on your back in the starting position—all while still balancing all the books on your hands and feet. Yes, it sounds impossible, but take it slow. As you start to roll your body to the side, think through the next action, what each limb will have to do in order to keep the books balanced as you roll. What position must you twist your arms and legs into to keep the books from falling? Everyone does this last step differently. Do what works for you. Think. Center. Explore.

⚠ WARNING: This exercise may not technically get you high but it will make you more receptive to other highs in this book . . . as long as your dog doesn't try to hump your ribcage while trying it out. Pursue at your own volition.

DIMENSIONAL THINKING TEXT ALERTS

In a study done by Eric Klinger, Professor of Psychology Emeritus at the University of Minnesota, subjects were given a beeper that would ring at irregular intervals. When this beeper beeped, subjects were asked to write down whatever was on their minds. The basis of the study was to identify how and what the average human thinks throughout the day. Klinger discovered that subjects spent a staggering 50 percent of their waking hours in internal dialogue, that is, "talking to themselves."

Consider, half our waking life is lost in self-interaction, thinking, wondering, stressing—alone. Even when we are in the midst of conversing with others or working on a complicated task, we are at the same time talking to ourselves, asking ourselves questions, lost in our own worlds. We never realize how much time we spend in self-reflective talk, and even what it is exactly we are talking to ourselves about. Identifying the frequency and subject of these thoughts allows us access to our subconscious minds. It gets us high. Well, kind of. But it is fun and fascinating nonetheless.

Get High Now

Find a cohort with whom you'd like to experiment. Agree to send each other between and five and ten texts throughout the day at random times. When each of you gets a text, write down your exact thoughts at the very moment the text was received. Just a few sentences will do. Keep these notes. Do this for five days.

At the end of five days review your notes. You'll be amazed at how very abstract your thoughts are throughout the day: at work, in the dentist's office, breakin' off a piece of that KitKat bar, at home leafing through the latest Fingerhut catalog. Even when you're "busy" with one conscious task, your mind will be lost somewhere else, swimming in self-reflection. Dimensional Thinking Text Alerts make us aware of this internal dialogue, offering a weird and lonelyish context into the workings of our consciousness.

VOLUNTARY SILENCE

We live in the age of perpetual noise. It's literally making us sick (see Colored Noise, page 223). Now more than ever a respite in the arms of Sweet Lady Silence will not only clear your mind, it will soothe your soul.

Shutting up is nothing new. Silent meditations have been integral to Christianity, Islam, Buddhism, Quakerism, and many other religions. According to these varied religious practices, being silent will not only bring you closer to God but also to your own "true selves." The road of silence, for them, leads to the palace of wisdom.

Famed architect, designer, inventor, and utopian, Buckminster Fuller (1895–1983) refused to talk for over a year so that he could singly concentrate on what kind of man he was and what kind of man he wanted to become. He considered words as tools and believed that if he was going to use them effectively he would have to study them from the *inside* out. When Fuller emerged from his self-imposed silence about a year later, he became one of the most influential American writers, speakers, and thinkers of the twentieth century.

Get High Now

Zip it. As you save mental and physical energy by not speaking, your other senses will grow much more attune: colors will get brighter, sounds richer, dreams much more intense. Try this for a day. Your mind will thank you. (And so might your friends.)

GRANITE

For more than six thousand years, Hindus have looked to the Himalayan mountains for inspiration. As the foliage, species, climate, and the world constantly and violently transform around them over the years, the Himalayas—like their deity Shiva—stand unwavering, strong, and resilient. This is because the Himalayas are made of granite.

It takes millions of years for granite to be affected by the weather. This resilience has given the stone a mystical quality throughout history. Egyptians used it in their most sacred buildings—pyramids, sarcophagi, statues—many of which still stand today. Westerners followed. The Washington Monument, the world's tallest structure when it was completed in 1884, contains large amounts of granite.

It is not just the impregnability that has attracted so many to granite, but its radioactive quality. Averaging 10 to 20 parts per million in uranium, granite emits radiation into the atmosphere, so much so that villages built on granite have been reported in folklore as being seen miles away—literally glowing in the dark.

Get High Now

Find a slab of granite: a kitchen counter, a subway terminal floor, a natural outcropping in the woods. Lay on it. Feel the energy; touch eternity.

Fun Fact: *According to a July 2008* New York Times *article, some granite used in countertops is so rich in uranium that it can release damaging levels of radon gas, which is the second leading cause of lung cancer. Even minor amounts of radon (about 4 picocuries per liter of air) can increase your risk of cancer, the equivalent of smoking a half pack of cigarettes a day. Sure, get high now off granite, but perhaps don't make it a daily habit.*

OCONENETL

Aztecs were a fun-loving bunch: They used human heads as soccer balls, committed random villagers to sacrifices at sundown, chomped copious amounts of psychedelic mushrooms for "religious purposes," and fought constant bloody battles with whomever happened to be around. They were *dedicated.* They even hunted little birds called *oconenetl* and ate their raw flesh, all just to get high. This is what explorer Diego Munoz Camargo discovered in the sixteenth century while in Mexico documenting the Aztec culture. Unfortunately, Camargo never bothered to note exactly what the mystical oconenetl looked like.

Research by ethnobotanist Richard Schultes (1915–2001) in South America suggests the tales of the oconenetl are probably true. The feathers and skin of birds in the genus Pitohui (to which the oconenetl could belong) contain poisonous batrachotoxins, hallucinogenic steroidal alkaloids that have been found in the Melyrid beetle and poison dart frog. Author Richard

Rudley explains that some dogs in South America actually seek out pitohuis specifically to get a batrachotoxin high. And you thought dogs were dumb? They are. Though they most certainly get ripped off pitohui, dogs also often die from batrachotoxin poisoning.

Get High Now

Not knowing which bird the mystical oconenetl is proves to be a two-sided blessing: It unfortunately inhibits the birds' psychedelic powers from being utilized in modern chemistry, but also protects it from being hunted by college students traveling the Ruta Maya on spring break. We suggest next time you're in Mexico, go with a proven high: inhale some ants (page 22).

METRONOME HEARTBEAT CORRELATING

Ever wonder why people don't mind the sound of clicking clocks in their bedrooms, but the slightest outside sound will jolt them out of sleep? It's because the measured, predictable click of a clock—a fixed-rate metronome—gives our brains and consciousness a sense of control and comfort, a pace with which to gauge itself as our bodies slip into the vulnerable state of sleep. By syncing the body to the prescribed beat of a metronome and then changing that pace, we can lull ourselves into altered states of consciousness, change the rate in which our bodies function, and twist preconceived contexts in our minds. We can get high.

Get High Now

Step One: Obtain a metronome (or search for a free metronome download online). Take your pulse, by placing your hand over either your heart, wrist, or neck. (HighLab prefers hand over heart: It's easier, and we like to imagine we're in the 2072 Olympic awards ceremony, winning the gold medal for Most High.) Concentrate on the rhythm of your pulse. Count aloud as your heart beats: *one, two, three, four*. Literally, *feel* the beat.

Step Two: Turn the metronome on and adjust the tempo so that it is in perfect sync with your heartbeat. If your heart keeps beating a bit faster than the metronome, breathe slower, concentrate, make it slower. Become the beat. Once you have locked the metronome with your heart, set the bpm a few beats lower. Make your heart beat slower. Relax. *Really* relax. Close your eyes. Meditate on the beat. Breathe. Go a bit slower if you can. Slow. Down.

HighLab found this exercise deeply hypnotic after about seven minutes. Some claimed seeing soft flashes of light. Those who lasted fifteen minutes recalled feeling tranquilized afterward—and semi-robotic.

> **Fun Fact:** *Heart rates vary. While the average newborn's heart beats at about 130 beats-per-minute (bpm), an athlete can boast a resting rate in the 40s. Most of ours lie somewhere between 50 and 70 bpm—generally, the lower the resting bpm, the better shape you're in.*

GOLDFISH BREATH

An old classic. According to one HighLab member, his grandfather used to do this exercise while driving. His grandfather claimed if done for more than twenty minutes, it made him feel that his 1972 Maverick was actually *floating* over the road, and that he was the conductor of a 54-piece orchestra playing Krzysztof Penderecki's *Utrenja*, the disarming movement from the soundtrack of the 1980 horror movie *The Shining*. At stoplights his grandfather would raise his arms violently from the steering wheel and between Goldfish Breaths (see page 123) sing along with the crescendo: *screech, screech, screech.*

We later found out the HighLab member fabricated this story under the influence of his own Goldfish Breath–induced high. Yeah, it's that good.

Get High Now

Sit comfortably on the floor or in a chair. Form the letter **O** with your lips. Inhale as though you were trying to gulp orbs of air the size of a ping pong ball. Do this ten times very quickly and very deeply. On the tenth breath, try to *swallow* the air. Then exhale fluidly through both nostrils for the same amount of time it took you to inhale the **Goldfish Breaths** (a count of about ten.)

Repeat this exercise twenty times. You should feel a slight tingling in your face, a new alertness in your mind. That sound in your ears? Listen closely—it's grandpa, and he's playing your song: *screech, screech, screech!*

> **Fun Fact:** *Goldfish Breath is also an effective cure for hiccups. Try it, unless you are hiccupping to try to get high, in which case, continue forth, soldier.*

BENHAM'S DISK

Scientific explanations can be a letdown. Really, was anyone happier to learn that rainbows are not the homes of leprechauns with pots of gold, but optical illusions caused by refracted light? Are we better off knowing albinos are *not* holy children from the moon, just regular folks lacking melanin pigment?

Indeed, sometimes scientific explanations can disappoint, which makes it even more thrilling to find some mystical magic that researchers still can't explain. Like Benham's Disk. Introduced in 1894 by toymaker C. E. Benham, this black-and-white patterned disk is monochrome when stationary, but when spun, unleashes a flickering array of colors. What's weird is the colors seem entirely real, as though the disk were creating some sort of portal to another, fantastically hued world. And still, after over a century, nobody knows how or why it works.

Get High Now

Grocery List:

- CD
- Glue
- Penny
- Lighter
- Pliers
- Scissors

This high takes about five minutes of do-it-yourselfing.

Step One: Print out the Benham's Disk at Gethighnow.com.

Step Two: Glue the disk onto either side of a CD.

Step Three: Grab the penny with some pliers. Heat the penny until it is very hot, holding it above the lighter flame for about twenty seconds.

Step Four: Place the CD flat on the table, lifting an edge about three inches. Insert the hot penny perpendicularly into the clear plastic center of the CD. Hold the penny there. When the plastic has congealed (about fifteen seconds or so) let go.

Wait a few minutes for everything to cool off. Then, with the Benham's Disk pattern facing up, grab the penny with your fingers and spin the CD. Concentrate on the center of the disk. Soon, from the black-and-white image, colors will emerge. As the disk slows, these colors will change positions, tone, and intensity. Different people will see different colors. Long live mysticism.

A Note for Lazy Sods: On Gethighnow.com is an online version of Benham's Disk. Though not as cool, it will give you an idea of what you're missing.

DEVIL'S FORK

What kind of food does the Devil eat? Devil's food cake and deviled eggs? These seem so *obvious*. HighLab thinks it is something much more unexpected, and creepier, like cotton candy and Jujyfruits. Well, whatever it may be, we can rest assured ol' Mephisto is picking at it with the Devil's Fork.

Our minds first perceive this evil fork as a two-dimensional representation of a three-dimensional object, the same way we may perceive, say, a photograph of a real fork. Stare at the Devil's Fork for a few seconds and you'll realize something is amiss; it doesn't *line up*. It's because the three-dimensional aspects are combined with those of the two-dimensional in such a way as to confuse our perspective judgment. We react by flipping the image back and forth between two- and three-dimensionality. We get high.

Get High Now

After requisite tripping, try shading just the top layer of the Devil's Fork with a pen or pencil. Ouch! What's that painful picking in your brain? It's Satan and he's forking at the mind of someone who should spend less time scribbling in books and more time going to church. For shame, you little heathen!

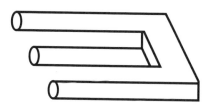

TRANSMITTAL BODY MUDRAS

The ancient cultures of Egypt and the Olmecs (Mexico) never had contact with one another, yet their pyramidal architecture is incredibly similar. Archaeologists have no explanations for this phenomenon other than that the two cultures must have felt some deep spiritual connection to the pyramid; perhaps it held some power unknown to us today.

Similarities between Egyptians and Olmecs extend beyond architecture into the religious poses of their statuary. The same highly detailed, almost identical postures found in Egypt and Mexico were also unearthed in other ancient cultures, from Africa to South America, Europe to Asia. Anthropologist and author Dr. Felicitas Goodman (1914–2005) suggests that the postures of religious statuary common throughout ancient cultures hold a kind of universal code as to how to reach a transcendental state. From these statues she developed a series of Transmittal Body Mudra meditation poses, each designed to alter the sitter's consciousness by tapping into ancient mystical energy. (Say it aloud: *Ancient Mystical Energy!*) A few of the most powerful poses are below.

Get High Now

HighLab assumed each of these poses for at least fifteen minutes. We found most only really got good after about seven minutes. Some members reported mild light flashes, increased heartbeat, and other psychedeliciousness. You'll see what we mean. Note that it is helpful to hold the postures while listening to Yucatecan Trance Induction Beats (page 84). Strike the pose, start the track, and prepare to get catapulted to a netherworld of spiritual strangeness— or just have your feet go numb. That's the fun of it. You never know what's going to happen.

WolfBoy

This posture has been discovered in prehistoric cave paintings from Australia to Siberia—both illustrating the stance with startlingly similar detail.

Get High Now

It ain't easy. While standing, place your feet about a foot apart with toes pointing forward. Bend your knees slightly. Hold your arms out at about 45-degree angles, relaxing your elbows so that your palms face backwards. Hold this position for fifteen minutes.

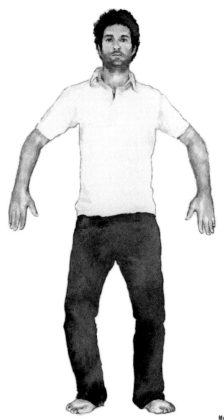

Coupled Energy Pose 👥

A seven-thousand-year-old figure in the Transmittal Energy Pose was found in what is now Romania. Similar figures were discovered throughout Europe and Africa, each dating from five to seven thousand years ago. According to Goodman, and Belinda Gore, author of the book *Ecstatic Body Postures*, this coupled posture provides an influx of energy to the female sitter and a feeling of transmitted power to the male. HighLab found these offered a mild trance state after fifteen (rather tortuous) minutes.

Get High Now

Female Posture: Sit on the floor. Extend your left leg out while bending the right leg. Reach your left arm across your body and place the tips of your fingers on the cap of your right knee. Bending your elbow, place the tips of your right hand on the same knee.

Male Posture: Sit on the floor, low stool, or pillows across—or to the side a few feet from—the female. Place your feet flat on the floor in front of you, about a foot apart. Place the palms of both hands beneath your chin, curling the fingers beneath your cheeks. Support your elbows on the knees. Relax your neck and face muscles, letting only your hands hold up your head.

Tongue Pose, a.k.a. "She's So Cold"

This pose dates from figures created somewhere around 300 B.C. to A.D. 800 . . . and around 1971, the year in which graphic artist John Pasche designed the famous Rolling Stones tongue-and-lips logo later featured on the cover of their annoyingly repetitious 1980 single "She's So Cold." For ancient Native Americans and prehistoric pagans, an extended tongue was a way to communicate with spirits. For Mick Jagger, it was a way to pick up butt-thonged Brazilian models. Though HighLab had no luck contacting Jah with this pose, or picking up butt-thonged models, we did manage to get saliva all over our newly polished hardwood floor. After five minutes we weren't sure if we had gone to a yoga hell or ecstatic heaven. Try it and decide for yourself.

Get High Now

Sit on the floor. Cross your legs, placing your right foot behind your bent left knee. Hold your right ankle with your left hand, your calf with your right hand. Keep your thumbs on the inside of your right leg, fingers facing forward. Open your mouth completely and extend your tongue as far as you can. Close your eyes. *You are the burning bush. You are the burning fire. You are the bleeding volcano.*

Romp of the Psychopomp

With uncontrollable vocal utterances!

A psychopomp is a soul guide who leads those who have recently died to the afterlife. Mythologies and religions all around the world share the psychopomp under various names and incarnations. Statues, figurines, and drawings from Central America, North America, Africa, and elsewhere share remarkable resemblances in the pose of their particular psychopomp. This same posture is still common in Africa as a pose of mourning for women trying to reach loved ones who have recently passed away. Depending on how superstitious or spiritual you are, this can be a powerful exercise. Sure hope you ain't 'fraid of no ghosts.

Get High Now

This is a standing posture. Place your feet about six inches apart, legs straight, with knees slightly bent. Cup your hands and place them behind each ear. Point your elbows away from your body. Hold your mouth open with your jaw relaxed. We strongly suggest Yucatecan Trance Induction Beats (at Gethighnow.com) for this pose. Start the track. As the drums begin pounding, sound an "aah." Allow any other vocalization to come from your mouth. Don't hold back. Consider that if you don't understand what you're saying, the spirits with whom you are communicating just might.

BASIL

Though it remains popular in the culinary arts, basil has developed an unfortunate reputation as a marijuana substitute, usually bought in dirty little plastic bags by unwitting high school students in front of suburban convenience stores. What's ironic is that if these little ne'er-do-wells knew that basil *actually* would get them high, perhaps they would approach the dude in the oversize Lakers jersey and baggy pants who just sold them the herb and instead of scolding him, simply thank him—thank him for giving them the opportunity to get *legally, naturally* ripped.

Basil contains high amounts of cineole (also known as eucalyptol), which, taken in low doses, can increase the flow of blood to the brain, resulting in higher levels of concentration, mental functioning, memory, and temporary relief from nervousness and fatigue. The magnesium and vitamin A in basil contributes to increased blood flow as well, relaxing the heart and blood vessels and helping to prevent cholesterol buildup. Basil is an anti-inflammatory and reduces headaches and other ailments in the same way aspirin and ibuprofen do (by inhibiting the cyclooxygenase enzyme in the body . . . blah blah blah). Basil makes us feel good.

Get High Now

A traditional Indian cure for stress and headaches is to chew about ten leaves of fresh basil. Not only will this mellow you out, it will clean your mouth: Basil is also a strong antiseptic and antibacterial. But if leaf chomping is a little too cow-like for your tastes, do as HighLab does: Just sprinkle some fresh basil on your next meal. HighLab's Test Kitchen found it goes great on top of Cranberry-and-Grand-Marnier-Glazed Pork Tenderloin or Oaxacan-style Albondigas Soup. E-mail us for the recipes.

PIROUETTE SILHOUETTE ◉

In this optical high created by Japanese designer Nobuyuki Kayahara, some people see the spinning dancer on her right leg spinning to the left; others see her on her left leg spinning to the right. If gazed at long enough, most will see her change direction, spin left for few moments, then right, and back.

The dancer is able to switch directions in our brains because she has no depth cues. The details defining the swinging direction of her arms, legs, and torso are too ambiguous for our visual system to understand. The brain, having such little information, starts making assumptions. It takes the information with which it is immediately presented and assumes a certain direction. However, if we concentrate on other details of the dancer that counter this assumed direction, the brain corrects the previous assumption and spins her in the opposite direction. Some people see her changing directions every few moments; for others it takes minutes. Some claim to never see it.

Fun Fact: *People with bipolar disorder will be slower to see the dancer change direction as their reversal rates in perception are generally more tightly fixed.*

Get High Now

Go to Gethighnow.com and click Pirouette Silhouette. Stare at the animated dancer. Within a few moments most will see her moving clockwise, then counterclockwise, and back and forth.

If you are having trouble seeing her spin in the opposite direction, concentrate on a different part of her body, or trace her projected foot with your finger and *tell* yourself she is moving in the opposite direction. The power of suggestion works wonders—as does the power of assumption, which is so strangely (and fascinatingly) demonstrated here.

KASSMAUL BREATHING

Special Super Negative-Feeling High

When your body builds up too much carbon dioxide it can enter a state of *respiratory acidosis*, which results in deep, inconsistent breathing. Adolph Kassmaul (1822–1902) named the condition after seeing it among patients with diabetes. Various health ailments can also cause Kassmaul Breathing, such as pulmonary or head injuries, or heavy use of depressant drugs like alcohol or opiates. People who suffer from Kassmaul Breathing report feeling claustrophobic, like being fish out of water—they constantly gulp and gulp for air but are never able to get enough to be comfortable. It's a terrible feeling. Let's try it.

Get High Now

Take a very shallow breath filling just the top of your chest. Exhale quickly. Wait ten seconds. Take another very shallow breath, trying to get air just past your throat but not into your lungs. Exhale quickly. Wait ten seconds and repeat. Now STOP. (Do not continue Kassmaul Breathing.)

What a horrible feeling. If continued, Kassmaul Breathing can lead to coma, even death. This high (rather *low*) should remind you to breathe properly. Try following Kassmaul Breathing with Qigong Diaphragmatic Breath (page 230) and feel the difference.

COMPRESSED TIME

In the late 1950s, psychiatrist Milton Erickson pioneered time-distortion hypnosis in which he attempted to rid patients of neuroses by either shrinking or extending their concept of time. His book *Time Distortion in Hypnosis* explores the discretions between the real and perceived time of incidents and provided ideas for therapy, such as how to abolish long-painful memories in seconds and make minutes of pleasure seem like hours.

Using Erickson's work as a reference, Stewart Brand (creator of the *Whole Earth Catalog* and current leader of the fantastic retro-future science think-tank the Long Now Foundation) conducted a compressed-time workshop at the Esalen Institute in Big Sur in 1969. In a single evening, he claimed, participants would experience the sleep, meals, and activities of a full weekend.

Get High Now

In the Compressed Time universe, an hour passes every five minutes. That means mealtime is every fifteen minutes or so; sleep is relegated to twenty minutes every hour. Though a three-day compressed-time workshop offers the maximum time-distortion perception, we know you have other things to do than eating twelve dinners a day. To do a simple six-hour Compressed Time exercise, go to Gethighnow.com and follow the directions. (The directions, though simple, are wordy—we thought we'd save some trees.)

Note: For those who attempt compressed time, the first couple hours will be the most difficult. Halfway through the workshop, however, you'll likely be amazed at how quickly your body and mind adjust to the compressed time schedule. If possible, try extending Compressed Time into a 12-hour session, even a 24-hour session. It's then that things get really weird: Your metabolism adjusts to your miniday, you get tired every forty minutes, time remains linear but becomes totally distorted. At the end of any Compressed Time session, be sure to allow yourself plenty of rest time the following day. In Brand's six-hour Compressed Time workshop at Esalen, most people needed 24 hours to adjust to "normal" daily schedules!

TURKEY LIVERS

The latest wonder nutrient to be celebrated by "natural healers," *choline* is prized for boosting memory, intelligence, and mood, among other things. This is accomplished through acetylcholine, a neurotransmitter that activates areas of the brain that choline helps to produce.

You ask: *But if choline is supposed to make you so smart, how come so many people wearing shiny tan braided belts are taking it?*

HighLab replies: Some questions we can't answer.

You: *More to the point: Why are you filling up valuable space in this incredible book with bad jokes about braided belts when you're supposed to be making us* high?!?

HighLab: *Exhibit A:* Choline increases memory and stimulates the brain to make you more receptive to lucid dreams (page 99). As we've already discussed, lucid dreams are undoubtedly some of the most psychedelic experiences you can have, with or without drugs. Choline is especially effective when taken in conjunction with the supplement galantamine, an alkaloid used in the treatment of Alzheimer's disease, which is made from (thanks for asking) the bulbs of Caucasian snowdrop flowers and select lilies.

The galantamine/choline one-two punch is used to also induce out-of-body experiences. Natural health food stores offer galantamine/choline supplements for this expressed purpose. A study conducted by Sitaran et al. in 1978 (published in *Science*), as well as other studies, have found extended use of choline to have positive results in increasing memory function. Insert your own having-a-good-memory-helps-you-to-remember-to-get-*high*-more-often joke here.

You: *Thanks, HighLab, that was both educating and fascinating! But what the hell does all this have to do with* turkey livers?

Well, lecithin, the compound used to hold commercial chocolate together, is made from eggs or soy, and it contains choline.

But you'll need to eat a few dozen Reggie Bars to reap the benefits. Luckily, bounteous amounts of choline occur in other foods.

Get High Now

Next time you're at Denny's, fill up on Moon Over My Hammies and *turkey livers*. Not only will you improve your memory and increase your chances of having a lucid dream or out-of-body experience, you'll be eating at Denny's, which will then greatly increase your chances of befriending an ex-con or pregnant teen. We're not sure where all of this going. We'll stop here.

LOCI METHOD

The *Encyclopedia Britannica* would probably classify the Loci Method as more of a memory-association exercise than a "high," but then again it lists a tomato as a fruit, and that just seems wrong. Either way, if the Loci Method doesn't get you high, it will allow you more thorough recall of other super-effective methods in this book. And being able to better remember allows you to remember to get high *all the time*—something you should never forget.

The Loci Method was invented by Simonides, a Greek poet (556–468 B.C.) who, after being the only survivor in an earthquake, was asked to identify the deceased companions with whom he had been dining when the catastrophe struck. He did this by imagining where each guest had been sitting at the dining table. It is, according to some, from the Loci Method that the expression "in the first place" comes.

It works by embedding "tags" (list items) within the established, multiple neural pathways we have in the memory of familiar locations. If one of these pathways tied to a familiar location is broken, we have several others to fall back on.

The Loci Method has been used to aid in the ordered recall of lists, first with Roman orators and today with politicians, business folk, or anyone else who wants to be less forgetful. You can also use the Loci Method to get high, or, rather, remember to get high *all the time*—something you should never forget. Are we repeating ourselves? We are. We should have used the Loci Method to organize our thoughts before writing this, and in doing so, would have followed these steps.

> **Fun Fact**: *In the brain is a massive network of neurons, which act by constructing pathways to the areas of our brain that store memories. Familiar locations have many neural pathways: One pathway may be wired to the smell of the familiar location, another may be wired to how the location looked, etc. This is why these locations are memorable—the many neural pathways make these memories easy to access. Less significant locations are harder to recall because we have fewer neural pathways to them. Neural pathways can break for various reasons. When all neural pathways to a location in the brain break, we cannot access the memory to which they were once wired and the memory is lost. This is how we forget things.*

Get High Now

Choose a Path: Go into your living room. Walk in a circle around the room, identifying ten pieces of furniture that grab your attention. These will be your markers. Walk around again, looking at those ten pieces. Repeat this one more time. Make sure the sequence of items is intuitive and easy to remember—this is the most important step in the Loci Method. Then, as you walk through a fourth time, give each piece of furniture a sequential number beginning with 1 and ending in 10. For instance, your order may be 1 = *sofa*, 2 = *chair*, 3 = *piano*, 4 = *stereo speaker*, etc.

Distribute List Items: You will use these pieces of furniture as markers throughout the room to remember lists. We'll demonstrate how it works with list items from HighLab's weekly grocery list: 1) Six-pack of tallboy Colt 45s; 2) a durian fruit; 3) liverwurst; 4) toilet paper. Using the Loci Method to remember this list, we will visualize that we are walking through the room passing each piece of furniture. On each piece of furniture we will imagine a list item: *1 sofa* = **six-pack of Colt 45s**; *2 chair* = **durian fruit**; *3 piano* = **liverwurst**; *4 stereo speaker* = **toilet paper**, etc.

Tie it Together with a Story: Now make up a story of how the list item fits within the room. Visualize that the items on each piece of furniture—the more unique and memorable the association, the better. This story/visualization worked for us:

> *I hope that* **Colt 45** *doesn't fall through the crack in the sofa, and I don't prong my ass on that* **spiky durian fruit** *on that chair. How delicious to cover with* **liverwurst** *the keys of my piano, then practice seven-octave glissandos with my tongue, etc.*

When you are done creating the story, flash back across the room, associating each item in its location again. This should take about ten seconds. If ever you get stuck, just start from the beginning piece of furniture and talk yourself through it.

The Loci Method is challenging at first because you will have to remember not only the order of the furniture items in the living room, but also their associated list item. Stick with it. Once your "path" is set, the rest is easy—all you'll need to do to remember anything is just imagine you're looking around your living room, seeing all the list items upon the furniture.

Funner Fact: *Three-time World Memory Champion Andi Bell used a variation on the Loci Method to memorize the exact order of 520 playing cards! First Bell chose a very familiar location: a walking path around London landmarks. Next, he visualized each card as a picture, animal, or object. He then imagined these card-visualizations placed along his familiar walking path. When he needed to recall them, he headed out into the streets of London in his mind.*

SINKING EDGES

This illusionary high works the same as Troxler's Fading (page 103). After a few seconds of staring at the dot in the middle of this image, the neurons that control our peripheral vision begin to turn off; our vision gets centered on the dot. When this happens, the outside grey walls of the circle begin to shrink then eventually disappear. Simple, yes, but it's kind of cool.

Get High Now

Stare at the dot in the middle. Keep staring. Watch the borders slowly slip away. Keep staring. Keep . . .

LETTUCE

The difference between lettuce and other alleged high-inducing household fruits and vegetables—like banana peels or peanut skins—is that lettuce actually, *really* gets you high. This is because the lactucarium present in several species of common lettuces produces a mild, euphoric feeling so similar to opium that in the late eighteenth century it earned the name "Lettuce Opium." In the early 1900s, lozenges and syrups made from lettuce were popular sedatives.

Unlike traditional opium, which is made from the addictive sap of the poppy flower, lettuce was promoted as being nonaddicting and much gentler in its effects. Ironically, it's the mellowness of the lettuce high that turned off the hundreds of thousands of self-professed "laid back" hippies in the 1970s, who often mixed it with catnip (page 221) to catch a mellow buzz. Many of these hippies soon moved on to more intense and destructive drugs—right before they moved into the Betty Ford Clinic. But hippies are silly. You aren't. Eat your lettuce.

Get High Now

Though there is no scientific data to support it, rumor has it that smoking wild prickly lettuce and the hearts and roots of iceberg lettuce can actually get you high. A neighbor of a HighLab member developed a standard preparation for smoking it. This doofus suggests blending the roots and hearts of iceberg or wild prickly lettuce, placing the pureed goop in a bowl, then evaporating it either in an oven, direct sun, or under a heat lamp. What remains is a sticky brown residue. Take this. Smoke this. There it is. A lettuce high.

HighLab: Getting Results

Not prone to smoking anything, HighLab attempted a lettuce high, just because it sounded so asinine. The initial problem was the preparation: We were never able to evaporate the water from the blended lettuce goop in the sun or an oven. After two desperate attempts, most of HighLab gave up, but one member was determined. She resolved to fire the blended lettuce mulch in our beautiful Le Creuset cast iron pan newly purchased from the massive royalties we received from this sure-to-be bestselling book. She then scraped the cooked lettuce, put it in a corncob pipe, and attempted to smoke it. She reported it tasted like "pancakes." We later discovered that the pan had been used to make blueberry flapjacks that morning and had not been washed. What this means: We're not sure. Good luck.

⚠ WARNING: Lactuca virosa varieties (known as wild or bitter lettuce) are poisonous. Avoid them. Stick with iceberg, "Canada Wild," or prickly lettuce varieties.

> **Fun Fact**: Science *magazine published an article in 1981 claiming that lettuce boasted 2 to 10 parts per billion of morphine. Great! Until you consider an average dose of morphine in a hospital is .5 to 50 parts per thousand of morphine, which is a* million times *more than lettuce.*

DIEKMAN CONTEMPLATIVE MEDITATION / MYSTICAL MEDITATIONS ⓢ

Achieving a mystical or spiritual state can be one of the most visceral, intense, and transcendent of human experiences. It's also ineffable, an indescribable sensation that is unique to each and every person who achieves it. For many, it's a feeling of pure, unified bliss.

Over the past 10,000 years, mystical states have been an essential part of almost every religion, from Hinduism to Christianity. Today, at least in the western world, these states are quickly becoming nonexistent. Most of us now have chosen to spend our time slaving at 60-hour workweeks, watching *The Wire*, or texting friends during long commutes. In the process, we've denied ourselves a basic human need: to see our lives through a larger, mystical lens in which we become fully conscious of our bodies, minds, and place on earth and in the universe. 'Tis true, brothers and sisters, 'tis true.

The problem for many nowadays is that achieving a mystical state is laborious. It takes a lot of practice, and the results are never guaranteed. It also usually involves religion, which many of us find unsavory. Arthur J. Diekman, an American psychologist, found it doesn't necessarily have to. In the late 1960s Diekman researched the ways ancient religions and cultures invoked such states. He concentrated on two ancient sources: Walter Hilton, a fourteenth-century Roman Catholic, and Pantanjali, a sixth-century yogi. Neither Hilton nor Pantanjali had contact with one another yet both shared startlingly similar methods. Diekman compounded these methods, calling them Contemplative Meditation, and developed his own step-by-step instructions for inducing mystical states within secular participants. It worked.

Diekman tested Contemplative Meditation on twelve people in an intensive multi-day study in which subjects were asked to look at a blue vase for about thirty minutes each session. In these sessions, two subjects claimed mystical experiences, including profound hallucinations and out-of-body experiences. In the fifth session one of these subjects saw the vase disappear completely. The other felt inextricably pulled toward it. By the end both had mystical experiences—without drugs, without suggestion. Just from taking the time to stop and stare for a while.

⚠ WARNING: This high is only for the true soul-searchers among us. It takes many hours and absolute patience. But consider that the end-effects could be life-changing, at least consciousness-changing.

Get High Now

This high is designed to give you the flavor of Contemplative Meditation, a conduit to the mystical experience. It requires you to concentrate on an object for an extended amount of time. You will simply be staring at the object, looking at it "as it exists in itself," without any other contemplations and without associations. You must try to avoid other thoughts and feelings during the exercises. The point is to concentrate all of your attention, *all* of your energy and awareness, on the glass, allowing it to fill your whole mind.

To view a truncated and adapted version of Diekman's original experiment, go to Gethighnow.com.

CAMBIATA ILLUSION ☺

This is a weird one. Audio experimenter Diana Deutsch developed this audio high to demonstrate how different people's brains can interpret the same pattern in a multitude of ways. What you will be hearing are two sets of notes playing simultaneously in each ear. These notes are opposite one another; as one high note sounds in one ear, a low note counters it in the other. Right-handers are likely to hear a higher pattern of notes on the right ear and a lower pattern on the left ear. For left-handers, the opposite. (Remember both right- and left-handers are hearing the exact same pattern played in the same ears.)

A small percentage of people don't hear high or low patterns at all, but alternating melodies and notes disconnecting in time with various stops. Some hear the two patterns in each ear and *another* pattern at the center of the head.

It all depends on how your brain is wired to perceive audio—everyone is slightly different. Cambiata Illusion and Deutsch's other audio highs demonstrate how the same sounds can be perceived totally differently from listener to listener, audience to audience, even ear to ear. It all seems impossible, and yet . . .

Get High Now

In the Cambiata Illusion link at Gethighnow.com, most people hear higher tones in one ear (right or left, depending as on previous page) and lower tones in the other. Listen to the track carefully, and try to figure out which pattern you hear, if it's a pattern at all. Remember, the pattern plays the same every time: It's our brains that perceive it differently. Now reverse the headphones on your ears, and play the clip again. How does it sound now? Most people will hear the *same* pattern in the same ears, even though these patterns have been juxtaposed when you flipped the headphones. Huh.

Bonus Fun

Listen again on your stereo speakers. Most people will hear a pattern of high three-tone melody that is close in pitch, and another melody that is similar but lower. As you play the pattern, shift the balance to the far left and then to the far right and the pattern becomes random and spotty. Shift it back to center and (to most of us) a pattern is again discernible.

MOZART EFFECT

The flowery flourishes. The sing-song melodies. The endless scales. To some, listening to Mozart is equivalent to watching a loudmouth magician do card tricks at a party. Only you can't kick Mozart in the balls, stomp on his magic cards, and steal his money to buy some Schizophrenic Blood (page 75). You are stuck with ol' Wolfgang, hearing his gauche and overwrought *pianissimo* in so many movies, restaurants, and snooty department stores.

In HighLab's opinion, Mozart blows. But at least he makes you smart. Or so said Rauscher, Shaw, and Ky, three researchers who published the effect of Mozart's music on the IQ in a 1993 issue of *Nature*. When testing subjects for spatial reasoning, Rauscher et al. exposed three different groups of 36 students to ten minutes of Mozart, silence, or relaxation instruction tapes.

Those listening to Mozart had an increase in their IQ scores of 8 or 9 points over others—a big jump. In a semi-related later test, three- and four-year-olds who took piano lessons for eight months scored over 30 percent higher in spatial reasoning than those given lessons in other areas.

> **Fun Fact:** *What is spatial reasoning? A person's ability to interpret and conceptualize spatial patterns through drawings and mental images, and visualize or change those images to fit various solutions.*

The Rauscher et al. study created such a stir in the 1990s that author Don Campbell wrote a book about it, *The Mozart Effect.* This spurred then-Governor of Georgia Zell Miller to pass a funding bill in 1998 that would provide every family of a newborn in the state with a tape or CD of classical music. Miller claimed the $105,000 a year to fund the bill was a small price to pay for providing infants and children with such a proven, effective learning aid. Distribution of the CD and tapes came shortly after but the impact of Miller's initiative is not predicted until 2017, at which time the citizens of Georgia will use their Mozart-enabled super-intelligence to do what their ancestors should have done generations ago: Move the hell out of Georgia.

Get High Now

While HighLab would rather be a Siamese twin of a loudmouth magician than listen to Mozart, you could give it a try, we suppose. The students in Rauscher's study listened to Mozart's Sonata for Two Pianos in D Major (K. 448). We suggest starting with ten minutes of that. Or you could just kick yourself in the balls.

⚠ WARNING: The Mozart Effect has since been contested. One report conducted by the Massachusetts General Hospital and Harvard Medical School looked at 16 previous Mozart studies, which involved 714 subjects. It found any increases in spatial reasoning to be statistically insignificant. And to think those hundreds of poor people were subjected to all that *sotto voce* for nothing!

TRANSFORMATIONAL KUNDALINI PITUITARY STIMULATOR [*Sa Ta Na Ma*]

If you are to do one meditation your whole life, this is it—or so say Kundalini yogis, the Hindu sect that originated in India around the eleventh century (see Kundalini Transcendent Chanting, page 36). Through its use of primitive sound repetitions, the *SA TA NA MA* chant was designed to clear our subconscious mind and provide us with a general feeling of wholeness. Some may even experience hallucinations. Kundalinis believe the chant activates the pituitary gland, the pea-size gland at the base of our brains that secretes hormones that help monitor blood pressure, growth, sexual function, and generally make us feel good. *Real* good.

Helpful Hint: The below are general guidelines onto which you can approximate your own schedule. Setting up a series of alarms is helpful when starting out. The goal is to make the exercise last for about thirty minutes. We know—it's long, but it's worth it. One High-Lab member experienced very vibrant visual hallucinations within fifteen minutes, so much so it scared her and she had to stop. Yes, this is deliciously powerful stuff. So put down the book and get to work. It's only a half-hour and, at a minimum, will clear your head of any negative thoughts and may give you a full mind/body high. You might even levitate. Find out.

Get High Now

Sit comfortably in a chair or on the floor.

Prepare: Close your eyes about 90 percent. (Or close them completely if that is more comfortable.) Breathe through your nose, inhaling to a count of about *five*, exhaling to *five*. With each inhale and exhale, concentrate your thoughts on the point between your eyebrows. Do this about three times.

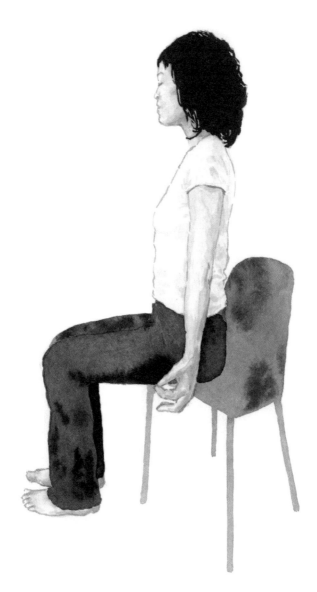

Chant: On the fourth exhale you will softly chant the phrase *SA TA NA MA*. With each syllable, press your thumbs on the flat section of your finger, that area opposite side your fingernails (where you pick up a pencil, for instance). Do this with the thumbs and fingers on both hands simultaneously, working from your forefingers to your pinkies. For instance, while saying *SA*, press your thumbs firmly against the index fingers; with *TA*, press the thumbs against the middle fingers; *NA*, against the ring fingers; *MA*, against the pinkies. Tell yourself you are sealing into your consciousness each syllable you speak with every press of the thumbs against your fingers.

Visualize: Additionally, as you say *SA*, visualize the syllable at the top of your head, *TA* in the middle of the head, *NA* a little lower, and *MA* exiting through the "third eye" between your eyebrows. Think of the entire phrase like an L pattern, starting at the top of your head, then leaving through the "third eye." Pushing the *MA* out is important—be sure to do it. Continue to press your fingers to your thumbs through every exercise listed below.

Suggested Times:

Minutes	Exercise
Five	Chant *SA TA NA MA* aloud, in your normal speaking voice.
Five	Whisper *SA TA NA MA*.
Ten	Silent chanting: Close your mouth and repeat the phrase to yourself, mouthing it with your tongue.
Five	Whisper *SA TA NA MA*.
Five	Chant *SA TA NA MA* aloud, in your normal speaking voice.
One	Listen to the mantra in your head. Then open your eyes.

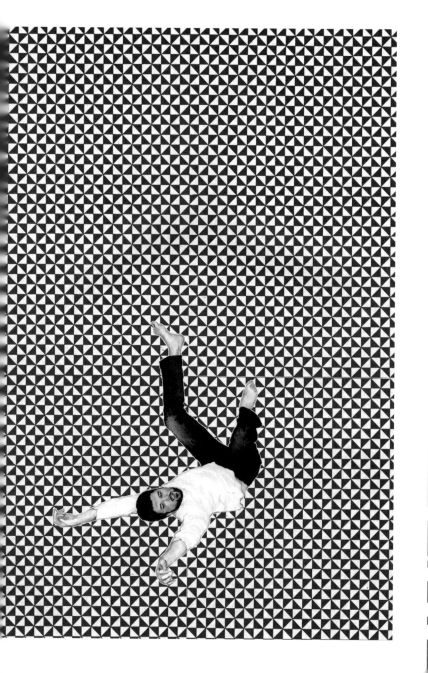

Chapter Three:

STIMULATING HIGHS

TWELVE-CYCLE METH BREATH

Yoga and meditation guru Leonard Orr first gained public recognition in the 1960s with "Rebirthing-Breathwork," a technique of rigorous breathing and meditation exercises that Orr believed could help people overcome the trauma of being born. By the early 1970s, an estimated 10 million people had "rebirthed" using Orr's method. Orr became so popular he ran for mayor of Los Angeles in 1973. He lost.

Today, Orr promotes physical immortality and the use of brain power to achieve wealth and fame, among other things. High-Lab can't vouch for any of Orr's teachings, but we can vouch for his various breath techniques, some of which can induce a quick and speedy stupor that can last for hours. Twelve-Cycle Meth Breath (our name, not his) is an Orr-based technique to give you energy at times when you feel tired or sleepy. It works just like methamphetamines, but without the facial scabs, rotted teeth, uncontrollably shifting eyes, urine-soaked off-label denim pants, stuttering, sunburnt necks, chain smoking, stick-up-the-butt walk, runny nose, oversize football jerseys, ratty hair, and suicidal self-loathing.

Get High Now

Sit comfortably in a chair or on the floor. Close your eyes.

Step One: Breathing through your nose, inhale four very short, very deep, and powerful breaths. Fill your lungs. Be sure that there is no pause between your inhales and exhales. Each breath in and out should last to the count of one.

Step Two: On the fifth breath, inhale very, very deeply, to the pit of your abdomen. Try to make it last to a count of about eight. Exhale completely to a count of about ten. Draw this breath in and out as hard and deeply as you can. Repeat again, starting at Step One.

Twelve-Cycle Meth Breath doesn't really get interesting until around the twelfth cycle (hence the name). But try to stick with it about 24 rounds. Go longer if you feel like it. Just bew careful when you finish—one HighLab member got so ripped off Twelve-Cycle Meth Breath he went out and bought an oversize San Francisco 49ers football jersey. Yes, it's that *methilicious.*

"KNEIPP CURE" HYDROSTIMULUS

Over 125 years ago, Father Sebastian Kneipp (1821–1897) was professing the wonders of herbalism, regular exercise, a diet of whole grains and vegetables, and feel-good spirituality way before it was cool and profitable. His Kneipbrød (Kneipp Bread) is still the most popular bread in Norway.

Some of his favorite holistic treatments were hydrotherapies. He wrote a book about them titled *My Water Cure*, in which he boasted the wondrous effects of water treatments on ailing patients.

Flashing was one of these treatments. It consisted of a patient taking a hot shower with intermittent cold-water blasts. Kneipp said exposing the body to heated water stimulates circulation, while the blast of cold water reinvigorates the organs and infuses the body with focused energy.

Focused energy, what? According to HighLab's doctor in residence (a real M.D.), what's really happening is that when you expose your body to any heat—hot water, hot air, etc.—the blood vessels close to the skin dilate. Bodies do this to cool off the blood in that area in order to maintain a consistent operating temperature of about 98.6 degrees. This is the reason our skin turns red when it is exposed to heat—the body is cycling blood along a more exposed area to cool it off. Radiators cool the engine of a car in the same way.

Now, cold water has the opposite effect. It constricts the blood vessels so that blood will flow from cold areas into our torsos to keep vital organs warm. The first areas the body takes blood from when we get chilly are the toes, fingers, and parts of our face. Lacking warm blood, these areas are first to get numb, turn blue, and in extreme cold situations, succumb to frostbite.

When you flash your body with alternating hot and cold water, you are rapidly dilating and contracting blood vessels, which alters the way your body normally routes blood. This provokes a physiological change in your body—if only on a minor scale. Kneipp and other therapists argue this physiological change is enough to stimulate the digestion and the nervous system, boost the immune system, as well as having other benefits. Flashing is still used today in medicine as an aid for several kinds of disorders, from spinal injuries to severe burns, depression to headaches, and is prized by athletes to improve fitness. It's used by others (smart people) to get high.

Get High Now

Shower as you normally would in hot water. Whenever you are ready, blast the cold water for one minute. Switch back to hot for about three minutes. Blast with cold for one minute. Try to do this cycle a total of three times. Trust Kneipp: Father knows best.

⚠ WARNING: Hydrostimulus is dangerous for those who are pregnant, diabetic, or have heart disease or asthma. Anyone with a chronic medical condition should consult a doctor before hydroizing. Use common sense; stop if you feel nauseous or light-headed.

TOADS (Do Not Do It)

Before Andrew Weil became the bearded, Gordon's Fisherman–looking "trusted health advisor" for millions of middle-aged upper-middle-class middle managers, he was a long-haired banshee-freak running through the Sonoran Desert getting wasted off toad venom. In a 1992 article for *Journal of Ethno-pharmacology*, he states that shortly after smoking the venom he experienced "profound alteration of consciousness within a few seconds of exhaling," after which he felt "slow" and "velvety." Wow.

What Weil and his fellow toadies sought was the intense five-minute high that came from the venom of the *Bufo alvarius* toad, wherein lurks extremely high concentrations of the hallucinogen 5-MeO-DMT. Contrary to popular myth, *licking* the toad won't work: The *Bufo alvarius* venom is poisonous, and ingesting it would most likely induce violent body convulsions and even death. To get high one must smoke it.

Since Weil's romps through the desert, hundreds, even thousands, have swarmed the Sonoran to smoke toad venom. *Bufo* smokers describe the high as bone-shiveringly intense. Larry Gallagher, a journalist and former Buddhist monk, was one of them. He wrote a feature for *Details* magazine in 1994 about his experience tracking down the *Bufo* and smoking its venom. Of his many revelations, Gallagher writes the toad induced "the most overwhelming cyclone of energy ever to rip through my brain, and it lasts for an eternity."

Get High Now

First stop, Arizona. Last stop, the mortuary. Do not do it.

CHRONOSYNCLASTIC INFUNDIBULUM
(a.k.a. Rotating Snake)

This visual high was developed by psychology professor Akiyoshi Kitaoka of Ritsumeikan University, Kyoto, Japan. Kitaoka theorizes that when our eyes see alternating light and dark shades of color in a particular order, such as in this illusion, they will naturally assume a prescribed route of motion within the object on which they are concentrating. (See related visual high, Peripheral Drift, page 234).

Kitaoka and other psychologists argue that our eyes will assume a righthand motion when processing the black and dark

grey patches in this illusion, and a lefthand motion when processing the white blocks. Because Chronosynclastic Infundibulum has so many varying patches in so many shades and shapes, the eyes become overwhelmed. They start assuming directions right and left in all the circles, trying to make sense of it all. If we concentrate on one spot of the pattern long enough, the eyes will eventually process all the information. You'll know this when the motion of the circles will appear to slow and then stop completely. To get the motion started again, all we need to do is re-overwhelm the eyes by shifting our focus around the page. You'll soon be caught in an endless cycle of wrong assumptions and right corrections, of stationary spirals appearing to be animated, alive, and in constant stop-start motion.

Though Kitaoka's theory sounds logical, the fact is nobody has unequivocal proof of why exactly Chronosynclastic Infundibulum works. What we *do* know is that it is very, very intoxicating.

Get High Now

Stare if you dare. (Also view online at Gethighnow.com.)

⚠ WARNING: This high can cause extreme dizziness and could provoke epileptic seizures. If while staring at this you feel very dizzy, immediately look away and cover one eye. *Do not close both eyes!* Doing so could prolong and increase the intensity of the attack. We're serious.

PRIMALING (Starter Exercise)

This is a form of therapy exercises developed by American Psychologist Dr. Arthur Janov in the mid-1960s. Janov claimed that most mental illnesses were rooted in childhood pain. By exposing patients to this pain in therapy sessions, Janov argued he could free people of neurosis and allow them to lead healthier, happier lives.

Primaling gained popular attention in 1970 when John Lennon began sessions with Janov. Lennon's subsequent recording,

John Lennon/Plastic Ono Band, was strongly influenced by these Primaling therapy sessions. Years later, other rockers, including Tears for Fears, also adopted Primaling.

Special Note: Primaling is an intensive therapy in which participants need multiple sessions before they gain any sort of positive change. Sessions revolve around seven steps: initiation, alienation, despair, acceptance, expansion, integration, and disengagement—which could all be titles of Joy Division songs. The goal of Primaling is to chip the self down to a "primal" level and build back up to a stronger, clearer, more "whole" you. Think of it like wiping a computer hard drive clean and reinstalling new software, but, like, with your mind, body, and soul. The instructions below are just baby steps to what is a large and complex (and at times wildly weird) process.

Get High Now

Janov heard his first "primal scream" from a man lying on the floor during a therapy session in the mid-1960s. The experience changed Janov's life. It can change yours, too. Maybe.

Step One: Go somewhere quiet where you won't be heard. Lie on the ground in a fetal position. Breathe deeply. Scream. Reach deep inside for your real self. Do it again. Now let your body and mind be free to do what it will: squirm, convulse. Tell yourself you are painfully alone. Scream. Be completely unhindered. Forget where you are, who you are. *Shout, Shout: Let it all out.*

Step Two: Primal on the floor for as long as is comfortable, or rather uncomfortable, perhaps two or three minutes. Do it longer if you can bear it. When you finish, lie on your back on the floor. Keep your eyes closed. Resign yourself to the fact that life can be painful, that all love can't be met or requited. Tell yourself that while you are an individual, you are also deeply connected to others in this world. Dwell on this for about thirty seconds. Consider that whoever you become it is impossible to fix problems in the past, to be the person you were before. Accept this as fact, as your motto. Think about it. Then focus on current tasks, current feelings, at being present in the world. Concentrate on all these thoughts for a minute or two, and when you feel ready, open your eyes. You are whole.

(And then go eat some salamanders, page 251, because all this hippie therapy stuff is getting way too heavy.)

NEGATIVE IONS

Nerdy contrarians chuckle when they explain that *positive* ions make us feel negative and *negative* ions make us positive. Whoever came up with this terminology should be shot . . . but oh, we say this just because we're feeling so negative from all the positive ionization in this room. Where we should be is outside, by the beach, beneath a waterfall. Because there, atoms and molecules are gaining and losing electrons, and in doing so are creating *ions*. Those ions that have *lost* an electron are known as positive ions; those that have *gained* an electron are negative. The largest quantities of negative ions are found within environments or weather patterns that have unstable or moving air. The rushing water in waterfalls, for instance, breaks water molecules into smaller drops, forcing the electrons to be knocked loose and to combine with oxygen atoms, which creates negative ions. According to ion-heads, when inhaled, negative ions will accelerate the delivery of oxygen to the cells, help boost the immune system, and increase serotonin, which relieves stress and gives us *positive* energy.

A cubic centimeter of fresh air contains about 1,500 ions. About 45 percent of them are negative, the rest positive. Ocean air contains about 2,000 negative ions per cubic centimeter. But the highest concentration of negative ions in the world is near waterfalls. Yosemite and Niagara boast the record: 100,000 negative ions per cubic centimeter!

Get High Now

Go sit by a waterfall for thirty minutes. Go sit by the ocean. Go.

ROADWORK

Part of the cardiovascular training of boxers and other athletes in the early to mid 20th century was to run long distances. Because this exercise often took place along the shoulders of highways and streets it became referred to as "roadwork." In the 1970s, more running tracks opened, requiring fewer people to run on the streets. Roadwork was renamed "jogging." Some (like us) have hypothesized that one of the reasons roadwork became so popular in the 1970s was that it induced upon its long-haired, knee-high sock-wearing participants a body-shivering, brain-thumping buzz known as "Runner's High." This high has attracted millions of people to "get to work" ever since.

In March 2008, researchers at the Technische Universität München and the University of Bonn in Germany reported after a two-hour run joggers showed a significant increase in endorphins—our bodies' feel-good opiates. The endorphins had attached themselves to the limbic and prefrontal cortices of the brain, two areas that control emotion. This significantly boosted the moods of the runners. It made them high.

A different study from Georgia Tech completed in 2004 linked roadwork with the body's natural production of the endocannabinoid anandamide, a neurotransmitter found in animal organs as well as foods such as sea urchin roe and chocolate. Endocannabinoid anandamide is a chemical cousin of THC, the ingredient in marijuana that has kept *Dark Side of the Moon* constantly playing in dorm rooms for over 30 years. In the small quantities in which it occurs in foods, anandamide is hardly noticeable; however, in the larger quantities, like those believed to be produced in the body during extended roadwork, some scientists believe anandamide produces a similar high to that of marijuana. (Some parts of Georgia Tech's research counter the *marijuana* theory, reporting that the presence of anandamide could not necessarily be linked to the alleged roadwork "high.")

Get High Now

The 2008 German study showed a boost in endorphins after a two-hour run, which seems like a lot of work for most people. In most cases (depending on weight and fitness) health improvements and the "runner's high" can be induced after about forty minutes. The high usually increases the longer you work. Note that these benefits are not exclusive to roadwork—most forms of cardiovascular exercise will make you healthier and high. All you need to do is get to *work*.

> **Fun Fact**: *Roadwork has been proven to reduce the risk of stroke and breast cancer and helps lessen the effects of osteoporosis, diabetes, and hypertension. It also lowers standing blood pressure and strengthens the heart, raises HDL cholesterol (da good shit), and increases lung capacity, which helps the body receive more oxygen. It's even been linked to the production of human growth hormone, which keeps young, great-looking people looking young and great.*

RISSET RHYTHM

French electronic music experimenter Jean-Claude Risset based this audio high on the Shepard Tones (page 38), the looped notes that sound as if they are constantly increasing or decreasing in pitch even though they are just repeating. Risset duplicated Shepard Tones in rhythmic form. The result is a drum-based track that sounds as though it gets faster and faster when, in actuality, it is playing the same steady beat.

To get an idea of how Risset Rhythm works we'll need to review how our brains process sound. Consider the brain as a famously impulsive file clerk who can't stand to have information just sitting around, clogging up its synapses. As such, when information comes in, the brain quickly places it in what it considers to be the most appropriate "file" to make room for new input. When the brain gets bits of information that don't fit exactly into a prescribed file, it makes an assumption, throwing this information into a file that it considers "close enough." Sometimes the brain misplaces information into the wrong file. These wrong assumptions, or "file" placements, are why we mistake visual, audio, or other sensory details: why we think a prick of a needle on a couch is an insect bite, the voice on the other end of phone line is your current girlfriend not your *ex*-girlfriend, etc.

The brain can make these same wrong assumptions with rhythms as well. When we hear any repeated pattern of sounds the brain will immediately try to place the pattern into a *rhythm file*, even if this pattern is random and doesn't perfectly fit. In this *rhythm file* the brain will attempt to put the pattern in a logical sequence of beats. Risset Rhythm takes advantage of these incorrect assumptions. The result is an audio high that sounds as if the same looped rhythm pattern is constantly speeding up.

Get High Now

In this audio high, slow drumbeats are faded out while faster beats are faded in. This pattern repeats over and over, faster beats fading to slower beats to faster beats, etc. The brain doesn't notice these subtle transitions between the faster to slower beats but attaches onto the *loudest* of the similar patterns of drumbeats. Risset Rhythm manipulates the volume in each of the fast and slow beats so that we cannot distinguish one from the other. As a result, we hear the Risset Rhythm loop as a continuous pattern, one that is constantly getting faster and faster, and yet never really seeming to increase in beat. It's a jaw-droppingly confusing and totally maddening illusion.

Headphones help but aren't required. Click the track at Gethighnow .com. Click play and hold on.

PUFFER FISH

Zombies have been around as long as . . . oh, who knows. Zombies are a myth perpetuated by popular culture, right? Well, tell that to Zora Neale Hurston (1891–1960), famed American writer, who traveled to Haiti in 1937 and claimed to have seen zombies firsthand. In the 1980s, ethnobiologist Wade Davis has also reported seeing zombies in Haiti, as recorded in his book *The Serpent and the Rainbow*.

Hurston and Davis didn't attribute zombism to any religious or supernatural tenets; they attributed it to the puffer fish. If administered in the exact amount, the tetrodotoxin of the puffer fish's internal organs purportedly induces a zombie-like state to the person who ingested it. After taking "just the right amount" of a puffer's tetrodotoxin, a "zombie" can stay in a debilitated state for days at a time. Additionally, anthropologists and researchers have bickered that the tetrodotoxin in puffers may also contain enough DMT (the powerful psychedelic) to provoke hallucinations. For Haitian witchdoctors, puffer fish offer a two-for-one: Not only can it dope an enemy into a zombie state, but it will also give them mind-bending visions while paralyzed. Neat!

Get High Now

Go to Haiti. Eat puffer fish. Get high, die, and/or become undead.

Fun Fact: *Tetrodotoxin is the same ingredient found in the fugu, the Japanese sushi specialty that gives people a loony high, including light-headedness, numbness of the lips, and a general feeling of intoxication. Improperly prepared fugu also kills hundreds of people in Japan every year. Both fugu and puffers are in the Tetraodontidae family of fish.*

BRAINWAVE MACHINES

These devices use goggles with pre-programmed flashing light patterns and headphones with sound loops to alter the rhythm of the brain into altered states of consciousness. In the 1960s and 1970s they were all the rage: Scientists celebrated them for their ability to induce different moods with the flick of the switch; hippies liked them because they mimicked the full visual and sensory effects of psychedelic drugs—but without all those conversations with lampposts knowin', flowers growin', and the morningtime droppin' all its petals on me.

In the 1980s, brainwave machines all but disappeared as well-intentioned but useless relics of a bygone free-living era. Today, they are back. Sold at Skymall, Sharper Image, and elsewhere, brainwave machines have been repackaged for corporate go-getters looking to boost their confidence, creativity, and energy levels. It's all in the *catecholamines* that some manufacturers claim the machines can spur the body to release after extended use. Catecholamines are chemical compounds that include adrenaline and dopamine, two neurotransmitters that make us feel good and help regulate body functions. Now, if brainwave machines could only teach these corporate superstars that hair gel, fleece vests, and tasseled loafers won't help them get "laid" by "hotties."

Get High Now
(or in two weeks delivery time)

Dozens of brainwave machines are available online and range from about $150 to $300. When calling to place your order, be sure to tell the operator that HighLab sent you and you'll get a special bonus—thirty seconds of awkward silence.

Do brainwave machines sound too infomercially fantastic to be true? HighLab thought so until we tried a couple out. We found the self-improvement claims for the machine spurious—they did *not* make us "more productive in sales and sharper at meetings." (The fact that no member of HighLab sells stuff, attends meetings, or is even vaguely productive to begin with is totally irrelevant, thank you.)

With that, brainwave machines unequivocally did indeed make us higher than shithouse rats. The Mind's Eye by Theta Technologies offered "50 different brainwave presets" and included some truly cosmic audio and visuals. One HighLab member said after a twenty-minute session on the Delta-wave setting that she felt "thick." Another reported expansive and sometimes scary "soul hallucinations." Wow.

Our trial of the Photosonix Innerpulse Light and Sound Relaxation Machine was less dramatic, and traumatic. While more compact and less expensive, we found the Photosonix visual and audio programs lacked the intensity and clarity of those in the Mind's Eye.

FLORENTINE SELF-FLAGELLATION

Thirteenth-century Europe saw the rise of a number of Christian flagellant movements, in which followers believed that whipping themselves would bring them closer to the Lord. What these folks were really doing was increasing the stress level in their bodies, which spurs the pituitary gland and hypothalamus to release endorphins to our nerve cells, the same pain-numbing compounds that flood into our bloodstream when we reach orgasm.

While flagellation was condemned in the Catholic church in the fourteenth century (though the practice still exists in pockets of Latin America and the Philippines), BDSM types keep it alive, always inventing more elaborate flogging techniques. Florentine self-flagellation is a two-handed style named after the Florentine fighting style, which incorporates fighting with two weapons at once. HighLabs did not attempt this high (it is against our religions) but it has been reported by various BDSMers that Florentining will get you unwittingly, berzerkly high if done correctly. And if you don't first pass out.

Get High Now

For those of you not already into this bondage stuff and who don't own whips, go buy a pair of toilet bowl scrubbers. Then go sit in a backless chair or stool. It helps to take your shirt off, but we understand if you are a prude. Anyway, raise your hands above your head. *Achtung!* Begin!

Count One: Raise your right hand and strike behind your head diagonally, hitting the center of your back. Repeat with the left hand.

Count Two: Swing the left hand down around the right hip, striking your left hip area. Repeat with the right hand on the other side.

Count Three: Swing your right hand under your left armpit and strike the upper part of the back. Repeat on the other side.

Count Four: Swing your left hand over your left shoulder and down, striking the small of the back. Repeat on the other side.

Repeat the pattern. (Or not.)

WALKING POWER BREATH

We've all seen them: the ratted hair, wrinkled evening wear, sleepy eyes, runny makeup. They roam the streets in the early morning, usually on Saturdays and Sundays. They walk the Walk of Shame. They partied all night and the next morning they couldn't find a cab, or didn't have a bus transfer, or just needed the fresh air, so they pound the city streets on the way back to their communal apartments, bedecked in last night's ruffled vintage faux-leather coat, slumped head, slouching shoulders, pallid skin.

If only they knew how to turn their Walk of Shame into a Gambol of Gaiety—a new walk that will turn each footstep into a piston, charging their lethargic bodies with positive energy! Yes! Presenting: the Walking Power Breath!

Note: This exercise is designed to be done while walking leisurely—not hiking or running. Like love, HighLab found it awkward at first, then natural and easy.

Get High Now

As you walk, inhale until your lungs are completely full (to a count of *five* if you can), then exhale to the count of *eight*. Repeat ten times. Breathe normally for about a half minute and repeat as necessary. This exercise will increase the flow of blood to your brain and help set your body into a more meditative, natural rhythm. Eventually, work on inhaling to an eight-count and exhaling for ten counts and feel the benefits increase.

YOHIMBE

Used throughout Africa for centuries as a folk remedy for fevers, coughs, and leprosy, *yohimbe* is made from the bark of the evergreen tree of the same name. Though many of its traditional uses as a curative have been contested by scientists, yohimbe has recently been proven by the National Institutes of Health to greatly increase blood flow in the body, especially in the Benjamin Franklin (a.k.a. Don Johnson, Alfred Hitchcock, Ron Howard, Dr. Wang PhD, Rip Van Winkle, penis). It works so well that yohimbe is the only natural substance approved by the FDA as having an indication as an aphrodisiac. Other yohimbe reactions include an electric-like tingling feeling along the spine and a jittery high that can last from four to six hours. Higher doses produce strong hallucinations—but can also greatly increase blood pressure, leading to dizziness, nausea, insomnia, anxiety, rapid heartbeat, and worse.

Get High Now

Available at most health stores, yohimbe is usually sold as an extract or tincture. Following recommended dosage, HighLab found yohimbe produces a very powerful, semi-schizophrenic-feeling buzz. Effects included pounding heartbeat, slight shortness of breath, and facial tingling—and this was with recommended doses! Standing up posed particularly awkward problems for the men in the group. This was creatively solved when one member grabbed a pillow from the couch and placed it over his lap area. Others soon followed.

Very mild flashing-light hallucinations were reported by a few members after about an hour. *We could not fricking believe this stuff was legal.* The speedy aftereffects of yohimbe lasted deep into the night, making sleep a challenge. Be forewarned: It is terrible stuff!

HighLab does not condone even the recommended dosage of yohimbe. Be like us, stick to Russian Reindeer That Have Just Ingested Urine and Eaten Amanita Muscaria Mushrooms (page 231).

⚠ WARNING: Yohimbe blocks monoamine oxidase, the enzymes in our bodies that help break down serotonin, dopamine, and other vital neurotransmitters. People preparing to take yohimbe should avoid foods like cheese, red wine, liver, and other foods containing the compound tyramine. These foods may help increase the blood pressure in the body to unhealthy levels. Don't use yohimbe with nasal decongestants either. An easier solution: Just don't use it. It sucks.

ENIGMA ◉

It has been said that writing about music is like dancing to architecture. Which means it's an absurd task. Kind of like trying to capture in words the ecstatic feeling you'll get as you tickle your amygdalae with this visual present we bestow on you. Instead we'll tell you how it works and let you draw your own conclusions. Here goes:

Created in 1981 by artist Isia Leviant, the painting titled *Engima* has long stumped scientists. Nobody knew why the lines appeared to jitter, how the concentric circles could move, or what exactly it was that gave this two-dimensional illusion its appearance of depth. Why did we feel so sucked in to the painting? Then in November 2008, neuroscientists at Barrow Neurological Institute in Phoenix, Arizona, discovered most of the blame goes to the *microsaccades*, the tiny involuntary movements that occur naturally in the eyes at various times.

Barrow researchers gathered three subjects and placed each in a chair in front of *Enigma*. As subjects gazed into the psychedelic cluster of lines and circles, cameras took 500 pictures per second of their eyes. Subjects pressed a button when they noticed the lines in *Enigma* as stationary; they let go of the button when the lines began jittering again. What researchers found was that the painting appears to "jitter" when microsaccades increased; it appeared stationary as the microsaccades ceased. These involuntary movements in our eyes were, at least in part, giving *Enigma* its illusion of movement. What's interesting is that unlike most of the other visual highs in this book, *Enigma*'s effects are not generated solely in the brain. The eyes are also to blame . . . *those lyin' eyes!*

Get High Now

Click on *Enigma* at Gethighnow.com. Stare at the image for at least a minute. Watch as the lines get jittery around the circle, as the circles move up and down the line. Even weirder, most people see an alteration in the color of the circle after a few moments of intense staring. When you are done, stare at a white wall. Uh huh. What you see is a brilliant Negative Afterimage (page 227) of *Enigma*. Two HighLab members liked this visual high so much they started dancing . . . to architecture.

KUNDALINI SYNDROME

Around 400 B.C. Siddhartha Gautama, the founding figure of Buddhism, sat beneath a Bodhi tree and began meditating, vowing not to stir until he had found enlightenment. On the forty-ninth day he was enlightened, and soon after discovered the path to Nirvana.

Prolonged meditation not only boosts the "spirit," as it did with Buddha, it also transforms the mind and body. Research shows that just a few minutes of meditation can stir changes in blood pressure, pulse, and brainwaves. These physiological changes become more pronounced the longer and more deeply meditation is practiced, sometimes crescendo-ing in an altered state of consciousness. It's in these crescendos that some people experience "epiphanies," "enlightenment," or "nirvana."

For most, this is a positive, blissed-out experience; for others it can be terrifying, followed sometimes by horrific visions and physical trauma such as blindness and paralysis. Some yogis and researchers attribute these traumas to the build-up of kundalini, the energy they believe is stored in the chakras of our bodies. When this happens, it is known as the Kundalini Syndrome (see page 177).

According to Stuart Sovatsky, psychotherapist and "world expert in kundalini yoga," the chakras get agitated and need to release stored energy, but can't because they are blocked in some way. Blocked energy diverts back into the body creating intense hot and cold flashes, vibrating, violent changes in breathing, confusion, fear, anxiety, urges to self-mutilate, and, purportedly, even death!

Get High Now

Some yogis believe the intensity of the Kundalini Syndrome can be abated by regularly purifying the body with salt baths and sticking to a vegetarian diet. Good luck.

REPETITIVE TRANSCRANIAL MAGNETIC STIMULATION ♒

People have been getting high off electricity for millennia. In the first century, Roman physician Scribonius Largus (his real name) believed electricity could cure everything from gout to headaches. He'd tell patients to step on electric rays (torpedo fish) gathered from the Mediterranean. These rays, when provoked, then sent an electric shock through the feet of the patients of up to 220 volts. (Shit! That's the maximum power that comes out of a standard house outlet!)

Medicinal electricity regained favor in the early 1960s when scientists used it to charge the transcranial area of the human head in an attempt to cure various mental ailments. What's shocking (pun meticulously intended) is that transcranial magnetic stimulation actually works, and is considered an effective treatment for anxiety, drug addiction, insomnia, manic depression, and more. Even better, transcranial magnetic stimulation offers a mind-numbing buzz.

In treatments, Transcranial Magnetic Stimulation is usually given through a Cranial Electrotherapy Stimulation (CES) machine. The electric current delivered from the CES to the brain boosts the levels of serotonin and dopamine in the body, two feel-good neurotransmitters that can help put the body in a euphoric yet alert state. They can make us feel *electrified*.

Get High Now

CES equipment can only be prescribed by licensed providers. A few smaller scale versions are available online. HighLab has not tried these mail-order versions as we have heard their effects are mediocre at best. We suggest sitting around and hoping that you are soon diagnosed with anxiety and manic depression so that you can qualify for TMS therapy. No, no. Don't do this. Try Moth Larva, page 49, or Ants, page 22, instead.

PARKOUR

This is an exercise in which there are no rules, no laws, no teams, no time limits. Its roots date back to early twentieth-century France, when naval officer Georges Hébert popularized training military troops on *parcours du combattant*—obstacle courses through which personnel had to walk, run, jump, throw, and lift themselves, doing whatever it takes to just keep going.

In the past decade Parkour (which has the pretentious French motto, *l'art du déplacement*) has become an internationally established movement less affiliated with the military as it is with counterculture. Many now consider it an exercise of defiance and freedom in an overly constricting world. In fact, Parkour has grown so much as to now have its own vernacular, disciplines, followers, and festivals. It even has specific names for men and women: *traceurs* and *traceuses*.

Get High Now

Equilibre. Passement. Saut de bras. Just keep moving.

Fun Fact: *Unapologetic badass, outdoorsman, and U.S. president, Theodore "Teddy" Roosevelt was a famous parkourist, or traceur. During his presidency he would get bored (i.e., drunk) in the winter and early spring and lead dignitaries on "point to point" walks around Washington, D.C., starting off at one point and "not turning aside for anything," including a swim across the freezing Potomac and Rock Creek when the water was still partially covered with ice.* Etonnant!

MALADAPTIVE EXPRESSION PARTY ♊

The Trobriand (also called Kiriwina) Islands are located off the southeast coast of Papua New Guinea in the South Pacific. Isolated and untouristed, the indigenous Trobriand tribes still follow many of their traditional customs, one of which is the annual yam harvest, which occurs in late July every year. During this event, clans of village women force men from outside villages to have sex with them, a task they do with frequency and fervor. The bacchanalia continues for two weeks until the village chief calls the women home, and everyone resumes life as normal under an unwritten "don't ask, don't tell" policy.

Similar orgiastic outbursts take place all over the world—Mardi Gras in New Orleans, Carnaval in Brazil, etc.—right before Lent every year. In the United States, tens of thousands of people meet every year in the parched desert of Nevada to freak out at Burning Man. (You know who you are.) Starting in 200 B.C., the Greeks and Romans held wild, wine-infused orgies in honor of the god Bacchus up to five times a month. What all this means: Having a good old-fashioned no-holds-barred party is part of human nature. It has been practiced by millions of people throughout history, and is considered by many to be an effective way to release the build-up of subconscious emotions that could otherwise lead to anxiety, unreasonable behavior, stress, and other ailments.

Get High Now

Have a party. Lose a little control. (Be safe.)

Fun Fact: *All that unprotected, nonconsensual Trobriand sex must lead to a springtime boon of babies right? Not really. The Trobrianders believe that conception is controlled by island spirits and not related to sex. That's quaint and all but* *what has most likely dampened birthrates is the large amount of yams in the Trobriand diet. Yams contain phytoestrogens and sterols, two chemicals with contraceptive effects. (In the 1940s, chemist Russell Marker modeled the first contraceptive pill on wild yams from Veracruz, Mexico.) Fact is, considering their constant unprotected boinking, the Trobrianders had for thousands of years historically low birthrates. This only changed when imported bread and rice came into their diets, immediately after which birthrates skyrocketed.*

YE OLDE ZÖLLNER LINES

German astrophysicist Johann Karl Friedrich Zöllner (1834–1882) first experienced this visual high in a piece of dressmaking fabric. The numerous repeated lines in the herringbone pattern on the fabric aligned at perfect 45-degree angles, and appeared to converge and diverge after a while, twisting and turning into a cosmically distorted nest of psychedelic spindles.

There are numerous theories about how this visual high works, or rather, why our visual system has problems processing the Zöllner Lines accurately. One theory is that because the shorter lines are at such an angle to the longer lines, our brain processes the longer lines as nearer to us. This gives the Zöllner lines an impression of depth. Another theory is that the brain has a tendency to overestimate angles that are less than 90 degrees (math nerds call these *acute angles*). At the same time, the brain has a tendency to underestimate angles over 90 degrees but less than 180 degrees (*obtuse angles*). This all makes the longer lines and the shorter lines crossing them appear as though they are more perpendicular to one another than they really are. The brain then interprets these lines as slanted.

Though the herringbone pattern has been in and out fashion over the last 150 years, this freakish illusion remains and continues to stump us.

Get High Now

Stare at the pattern for a minimum of thirty seconds. The effect intensifies the longer you gaze. So quit reading this and *gaze*!

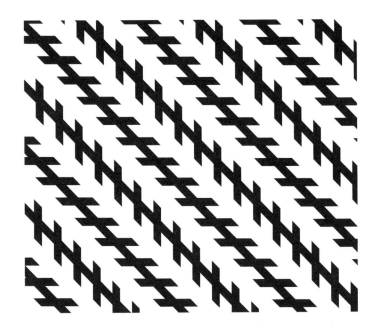

HOLOTROPIC BREATHING ☺

This breathing method seeks to unlock a world of whole consciousness that its inventor, Stanislov Grof, M.D., Ph.D., believes exists in all people. The original method comprised five elements—group work, intense breathing, music, body work, and drawing. Experiences that emerge through Holotropic Breathing are, according to Grof, identical to that of psychedelic drugs, including very intense and sometimes violent hallucinations.

It's not easy. Holotropic Breathing first strips subjects down, dragging them through "the dark night of the soul" before clothing them again in new, superconscious cloaks. The initial sessions are usually spent in "painful confrontation," a purging that builds to a critical climax after which most subjects experience a "mini-death-rebirth" experience. Exercises after this point are easier and often filled with various personal realizations. Participants report the Holotropic climax as being one of the most intense and cathartic experiences of their lives, on or off drugs. Reports of out-of-body experiences, spiritual awakening, and connectivity with the greater whole of earth are common.

⚠ WARNING: Holotropic Breathing is physically and mentally stressing. Use common sense: Do not attempt if you are pregnant, asthmatic, or have any pre-existing health conditions. The below is only an example of how a Holotropic session might work. Sample it if you'd like, but if at any time you feel uncomfortable in any way, stop immediately. We all have our limits: don't push them. There are over 1000 trained facilitators of Holotropic Breathing throughout the world. Consult one (as well as your doctor) before proceeding through an entire session.

Get High Now

Find a friend you trust and go to a quiet place where you won't be disturbed; turn off phones, alarms, etc. Your friend will not be interacting with this exercise; she is just there in case you may need assistance.

Holotropic Breathing is simple; what's challenging is its duration. To take full advantage of Holotropic's benefits, you must follow the exercise *all the way* through to the end. Holotropic practitioners argue that, as each person will have a markedly different experience, "ending" times will vary greatly.

Step One: Lie on a bed or on the floor. Dim the lights low. Breathe softly. Relax. After a minute, breathe heavier. Relax. Breathe deeper. Breathe from your mouth or nose—whatever is most comfortable. Do this for a minute or two.

Step Two: Breathe deeper now. Within 10 minutes most people feel some tensing of the lungs or tingling in the fingertips or cold spells.

Keep going. The tension will break; just keep breathing. Stay at this pace. Adjust your body or wrap yourself in a blanket if necessary. Practitioners argue that "resolution will come." Just keep going.

Most people experience climax about 40 minutes into this exercise. It is often preceded by intense geometric hallucinations and stars. This is a very emotional time for some people. When you are resolved (again, you will *know* when this time comes, they say) breathe normally. Let yourself come down. Stay in contact with your partner if you need help. Within 15 minutes your body should be functioning normally—though your mind will be in a very different, clear-headed and resolved space.

The effects of Holotropic Breathing can last up to two days and are often associated with extreme lucidity and a general feeling of levitation and bliss. This is one of the most powerful techniques a few members of HighLab ever experienced. Prepare yourself.

SKINNER RELEASING
(a.k.a. Petting Imaginary Animals Backwards)

Skinner Releasing is a dance therapy designed by Joan Skinner in the 1960s to reconnect us with animal grace, that intrinsic sense of balance, coordination, and agility we are all born with but lose as we grow older and integrate into the confines of modern society.

Skinner Releasing techniques helped spawn Contact Improvisation, the enormously popular 1970s improvisational dance in which dancers "jam" with walls, floors, chairs, or other people as "partners." Contact Improvisation is still practiced today in workshops worldwide and, informally, by fat dudes at bluegrass concerts.

Skinner Releasing coaches dancers to let go of inhibitions, confines, and controls, to move with our *innate* sense. One technique involves dancers meditating into trances to evoke visions from the subconscious. Devotees claim this and other Skinner techniques have numerous psychological benefits, including clearing the soul and integrating the body and mind in a perfect union.

Get High Now

Step One: Find a quiet room where nobody will bother you for about ten minutes. Stand in the middle of the room. Begin by tilting your neck back and forth softly. Now tilt it side to side. Shake one leg, trying to release the tension. Now do this to your other leg, then one arm, then the other. Keep a rhythm, moving it from limb to limb, side to side. While moving, feel the beat of your heart.

Step Two: After about a minute, start moving your torso—forward, backward, side to side. Find your own beat. Let your feet walk around on their own volition. Don't try to control them. They are free to go where they want and so are you.

Step Three: Move your whole body now: dance cat-like, dog-like, fat-dude-like—whatever feels most natural. Oh look! An imaginary dog has decided to dance with you. And here comes a cat. Pet the animals. Now pet them *backwards*. And feel them pet you. Yes, it tickles! Stick with it for at least five minutes.

Skinner Releasers claim they can reach ecstatic, orgiastic states within just a few minutes. Can you?

BEETLE WINGS

This *lytta vesicatoria* beetle, commonly known as the Spanish Fly, is famous in urban legends for inducing sexual desire in unwitting dates who eat it. The weird thing is it actually works. The key is in the cantharidin, a chemical compound that upon being consumed and urinated out of the body inflames the genitals and livens the libido.

Lytta vesicatoria wings have been used as aphrodisiacs throughout history. Hippocrates first recorded their medicinal use in the fourth century B.C.. In the first century A.D., Augustus Caesar's wife, Livia, dosed dinner guests with them. The Marquis de Sade used them on prostitutes (which seems kind of redundant), apparently to provoke them into various acts of sexual deviance, and so on . . .

Get High Now

Lytta vesicatoria wings are illegal in the United States except for use in animal husbandry or as a topical prescription (cantharidin can help heal some types of warts). HighLab has not experimented with *lytta vesicatoria* wings, as we are all either celibate or robustly virile.

For our more perverted friends who might consider munching them, be warned: The difference between a fun (a sexual healin' feelin') and unfun dose (a day-long boner and other nasty effects of satyriasis) is very thin. We suggest taking a trip to North Africa, where *lytta vesicatoria* wings can be found in everything from bread spreads to spices. Ask around, but remember: That bulge in a Moroccan spice vendor's pants does not mean he's just happy to see you.

AUTOSTEREOGRAM ◉

Popular in the 1990s, autostereograms are two-dimensional images of repeated patterns from which an embedded three-dimensional image appears to emerge after extended viewing.

When looking at an autostereogram, the brain receives repeating 2D patterns from both eyes, but can't match these patterns correctly. The brain tries to correct this by placing the embedded image at a depth different than the repeated two-dimensional images in the poster. When we eventually adjust our eyes to focus on *both* the embedded image and its surroundings, the only way for the brain to make sense of the image is to assume they are occurring in two different places, somehow separated from one another. This gives the autostereogram its three-dimensional appearance.

Get High Now

See the autostereogram at Gethighnow.com. Focus your vision on one small speck. Let it linger. Try to completely defocus your eyes on the rest of the picture. This sounds weird, but give it time and you'll see. Oh yes, you'll see.

BANANA PEELS

One of the most celebrated legal highs in the western world, banana peels, when smoked, offer the most revelatory and consciousness-twisting hallucinations and orgiastic full-body highs a human can experience.

Wrong.

No matter what your grandfather told you, you cannot get high off banana peels. Now go eat some betel nut (below).

Get High Now

. . . off of something else in this important book.

BETEL NUT

What tobacco is to the western world, betel nut is to Asia. This hard seed of the "betel palm" (*Areca catechu*) is so popular throughout the East that India has implemented new standards on who can buy it. The law prohibits all people under the age of five—*as in, children who are five years old!*—from purchasing betel. The impact of India's brave legislation is yet to be determined.

What attracts young and old alike to betel nut are its arecoline, guracine, and arecaidine, alkaloids that give chewers a mild sense of euphoria and alertness, and an energy boost. What repulses *everybody else* is the blood-red drool ribbons that plume uncontrollably from the mouths of these chewers—staining clothes, sidewalks, and anything else that comes within their paths. But most betel-nut heads couldn't care less; for them blood-red drool is all just part of a proud thousands-of-years-old tradition of getting high.

Get High Now

Betel nut is available dried, cured, or in raw form. Prepackaged varieties are available at most Asian markets. Traditional Indian hospitality often includes serving *paan* to guests. Paan consists of betel leaves (from the betel pepper vine, *Piper betel*, which also contain high-inducing alkaloids) wrapped around betel nuts, spices, and in some cases, tobacco. A preparation common throughout Oceania and Southeast Asia is to wrap chunks of the nut with a piece of lime in a betel leaf.

HighLab attempted the latter method but improvised mint leaves for betel pepper leaves. Reactions were mixed. Some members respected the mild clammy, sleazy, speedy high, comparing it to an overdose of cheap coffee. Others thought it more trouble than it was worth.

> **Fun Fact:** *Researchers found significantly increased heart rate within two minutes for those who chomped betel nut; the heart-pounding effects lasted about twenty minutes.*

⚠ WARNING: Betel nut is addictive and has been proven to promote oral cancer after repeated use. But we know you will not be using this sick stuff repeatedly . . . if at all.

OUCHI GOOCHI

I am dressed in tight white pants and a half-unbuttoned cream-colored polyester shirt from which a silk ascot plumes flower-like around the collar. I tap my Beatle boots in rhythm with the thumping tom-tom drum that echoes from a corner stage. There, Mo Tucker is hoisting mallets above a two-piece drum set. In front of her, Lou Reed, bedecked in wraparound spy glasses and black turtleneck, has just begun singing the opening lines of the haunting dirge, "Venus in Furs."

It is 1966, summertime in New York City, and it is hot. I have come with a group of beat poets from around Manhattan to the Gymnasium to attend Andy Warhol's debut of the Exploding Plastic Inevitable, a touring Pop Art party featuring Warhol, the Velvet Underground, and Nico. I am high. I am very high. Not from the amphetamines being injected randomly into the legs of passersby by short-skirted starlets, but from the enormous checkered pattern projected along a back wall. It is called the Ouchi Goochi.

This visual high was created by Japanese artist Hajime Ouchi in 1977. (Yes, a decade after we saw it at the Exploding Plastic Inevitable. Weird.) It works much the same way as other optical art highs—by tricking our visual system into perceiving motion, color, or distorted perspective within a stationary two-dimensional graphic.

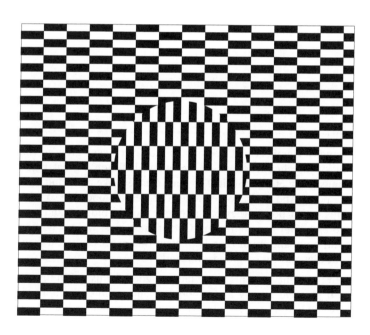

How specifically the disk at the center of this visual high appears three-dimensionally moving is not fully understood. One theory argues the disk itself jitters because the complex black-and-white pattern of tiles overwhelms the neurons in our eyes. Our visual systems try to stabilize the horizontal tile pattern with vertical motion, but overcompensate, and hence the disk appears to be moving right to left. The pattern outside the disk similarly overwhelms the eyes. These tiles are oriented vertically, so the visual system tries to stabilize the pattern horizontally but, again, overcompensates. This gives the area surrounded the disk its up-and-down motion. Now, since the disk and background appear to be moving independently of one another (up and down, right to left), our brain assumes they are separate objects. This (wrong) assumption gives Ouchi Goochi depth, creating the illusion that either the disk or its surrounding area is three-dimensional. Our overstimulated eyes keep it moving.

Get High Now

Just look at it, European Son. Shift focus from area to area to heighten the effects.

FAT

Crunchy Flamin' Hot Cheetos and Go-Gurt never grew in the murky marshes from which we evolved. When we eat these things many of us know it. They make us feel like poop and look like poop. And poop. Some modern processed foods are so injurious to our bodies they can alter our moods, biology, and psychology. They can depress us. One of the easiest ways of getting a full body-and-mind high is to strip this processed crud from your diet and eat *real* food—like fat!

In the right amounts some fats are good for us, providing us with physical energy and a boost of endorphins that normalizes and betters our moods. We know from previous highs how our bodies and minds feel when flush with endorphins: blissful, content, and wholly high. We also know how we feel when our bodies lack endorphins. Just ask any moody, cranky, pissy son of bitch. Nutritionists, including Nan Allison, attribute at least part of negative mood swings to a lack of fat in our diets.

Get High Now

Next time you're feeling down and troubled and need a helping hand, turn off the Carole King and gobble some healthy fatty foods like avocados, almonds, or oily fish like mackerel. Give yourself an endorphin rush . . . and enjoy the natural fat high.

⚠ WARNING: While delicious fatty foods like French fries, cheese sauces, and chocolate will indeed give us an endorphin rush, they can be harmful to our overall health if eaten consistently in large quantities.

HOLOPHONIC SOUND ⊚

Hugo Zuccarelli, an Argentine who dabbled in various sound experimentations in the 1980s, believed the human auditory system not only hears sound but emits sounds as well. The combination of these heard and emitted sounds form a reference pattern from which the brain can determine the direction a sound is coming from.

Zuccarelli based Holophonic Sound on this theory. In this recording technique, sound samples played through stereo speakers or headphones sound three-dimensional, as though they are not being amplified but actually occurring *all* around us. It's very odd.

Holophonic Sound is based on binaural recording, a technique in which stereo microphones are fixed within a prosthetic head—replete with ears and sinus cavities—to mimic the complex auditory system of the human head. (Doing this makes binaural recordings sound more natural and more realistic than normal stereo recordings because we hear the recordings with the same nuances we would hear sounds in real life within our own heads.) Zuccarelli recorded sound with the same multi-exposure premise as binaural recordings, but combined his recordings with "inaudible digital reference signals" that mimic the processes in the human auditory system. The resulting Holophonic Sound, when played through headphones, is so realistic and three-dimensional that it can often arouse other senses—smell, taste, and touch—within most people who listen to it. Allegedly, Holophonic Sounds can stimulate areas of the ear that normal recorded or real-life sounds cannot. For this reason, some people with hearing impairments whose brains cannot process other sounds can hear Holophonic Sound. HighLab found Holophonic Sound to be visceral, tactile, and altogether head-shakingly neat. Hear for yourself.

Get High Now

Zuccarelli released the album *Zuccarelli Holophonics* in 1983 to show off his technique, but good luck finding a copy. Other audio engineers have followed his techniques and developed some fascinating and strange recordings. Be sure to listen to any Holophonic recordings with headphones. Notice how the sound doesn't just jump from ear to ear like a traditional stereo recording, but actually circles in front and in back of the head. Go to Gethighnow.com to hear some.

RIGHT/LEFT BRAIN COUNTERINTUITION DISCOURSE

Try in the office!

This HighLab original language perception game plays with the intuitive functions housed in the right hemisphere of the brain, while simultaneously activating the sequential and analytical reasoning in the left hemisphere. That's right, you'll be using all of your mental faculties to sound like a total idiot. And you'll love every goddamned minute of it. You will. Here's how it works:

This is a game no one else has made up so we claim it as our own. Do you like it?

Notice how the above Right/Left Brain Counterintuition Discourse is entirely monosyllabic words. In this game, this is how you must speak for at least thirty minutes at a time—all in monosyllables. *Each one can talk with just one word at a time.* Sounds easy, right? Try it.

Get High Now

Use Right/Left Brain Counterintuition Discourse to:

Order a coffee: ("Can I have one cup of that brown stuff there? Yes, the drink for a mouth.")

Call a client: ("Hi, you. It is me. The man who talked to you in the past, to sell a thing. Hi there.")

Ask your boss for a raise: ("I work well. Please pay me more.")

It's much harder than it seems. Try it for a minimum of a half hour, especially if you're at work and about to go into a meeting or need to make a presentation. That thump-thump-thumping in your brain is the high you get from reversing your pre-set perceptions. Don't worry, you'll have plenty of time to recover. At home. Unemployed. Alone.

Fun Fact: *In the early 20th century, writers translated the text of a number of classic books into single syllables to make them more accessible to young readers. Among the works is J.C. Gorman's* Alice in Wonderland in Words of One Syllable *(1905), which is still available today.*

CENTAUR-LEVEL TRANSMOGRIFICATION

Half-human, half-horse, the centaur mythology dates from as far back as 3000 B.C. The myth was spawned when nomads first appeared riding horseback into villages whose denizens had yet to domesticate the horse. Villagers mistook the nomads as godlike half-animals because they had never before seen, nor could they imagine, a man *riding* a horse. In another interesting cocktail-party factoid, Aztecs thought the first Spanish cavalry-men centaurs as well, as Aztecs too had never considered the horse as a means of transportation.

But history is (*yawn*) in the past. We know you're interested only in the future, a future in which you are *high*. In this case you must, again, delve into some mystical hoo-ha. Hold on to your handwoven floppy hats: It's going to get cosmic.

Some parapsychologists argue that one of the most health-ful levels of human consciousness is at the "centaur level"—a state in which the psyche, like a centaur, is not a mere rider on a horse, but *a part* of the horse, in full control of both mind and body. Parapsychologists cite that through life most of us keep our minds intact but let our bodies go. Only when the body is sick or ailing do we notice it, nursing it back to health. When the body is healthy, we ignore it and wait until it gets sick again. We have become largely dissociated from our bodies on pur-pose because we fear their vulnerability and feel we are helpless toward their constant degrading. From the moment we are born we are dying. This thought spooks us.

Centaur-Level Transmogrification is an exercise developed to help dissolve this "mortality" block, to put the mind and body back in synchronization with one another. By enabling people to accept the fragility of the body, and of life itself—to accept that *everything* will eventually die—parapsychologists believe we can finally be resolved to accept ourselves.

Get High Now

Step One: Lie down on the floor. Close your eyes. Take a deep breath through your mouth or nose to the count of about *five*. Exhale. Take another deep breath. Feel your body. Don't try to feel anything in particular; just let your mind wander. How do your toes feel? Your arms? Can you feel your legs? Do you lose concentration? If you do, what are you thinking of?

Step Two: Breathe a few more breaths in and out. After about a minute, imagine your stomach is filled with a huge balloon, stretching from your abdomen to your throat. Breathe in, fill up the entire balloon. Let your stomach and chest expand. Inhale as deeply as you can, to a count of *five*, *six*, *seven*, or more.

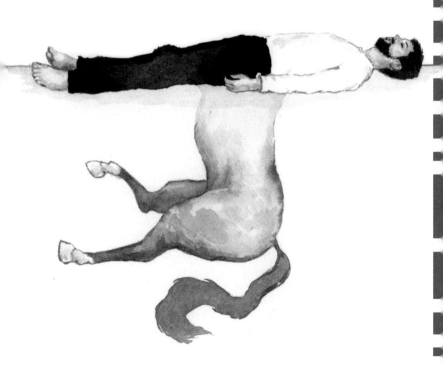

Step Three: While you are breathing, if you feel discomfort in your body, take note of the areas. These uncomfortable spots are your *blocks*. Concentrate your mind on one of them as you breathe deeply in and out. Use your mind to eliminate the blocks one by one. Parapsychologists believe these blocks are holding you back from being free, from accepting the living organism that is your body. Breathe. Work on each block, focusing on them one at a time while continuing to breathe.

The goal of Centaur-Level Transmogrification is to eventually liberate yourself of all these blocks. By doing this you will become in perfect tune with your body, accepting it in all its conditions and stages—even its constantly degrading state. You will then be ready to head into the Centaur Level. Then don thy horseshoed hooves and gallop forth, horseman—gallop forth!

ALPHABETICAL SEQUENCING ARTICULATION

Like Right/Left Brain Counterintuition Discourse (page 194), this HighLab original makes us aware of the linguistic process constantly percolating in our brains. To play, each player is required to replace the instinctual subconscious language process for a *conscious* one—painstakingly thinking through the first letter of each word in a sentence before speaking the next. Our brains don't normally operate like this, making this task difficult and provoking a disorienting, brain-baffling linguistic high. What's better, while playing, each volunteer will sound like a vacationing German in Mexico trying to order a taco by picking random phrases out of his Berlitz guide. Yes, you'll sound *that* sad and ridiculous. *Probieren Sie es jetzt, Arschloch!*

Get High Now

All the rules of Alphabetical Sequencing Articulation are simple. Because it's an easy game. Could you want to play it?

Notice how every sentence in the above line begins with the next letter in the alphabet—**A**ll the rules . . . **B**ecause, it's an easy . . . **C**ould you want . . . This is how to play Alphabetical Sequencing Articulation.

Try to speak this way to the next person that approaches you: "**A** good morning to you! **B**et you had fun this weekend. **C**an I see your socks, please?" Never tell anyone you are playing Alphabet Game. Just keep it your special secret. Try with friends.

Dining Tips from HighLab

Lets admit it, themed dinner parties are boring. *A Fondue Fiesta! South of the Border at Dave and Jen's Mexican Mixer! 1900s Food Night: Bring a Bottle of Moonshine!* Yawn. After our ninth such invitation this year, HighLab couldn't take it anymore. So we developed a theme for a dinner party guaranteed to keep us entertained—or at least give every guest a batty high. Here's how it works:

Invite six people to your house. Approach each secretively and say you want to play a little trick on the rest of the group. Then give each guest one of the below roles to follow. Convince this guest to stick with his particular role throughout the *entire* night, and that it must be kept a secret from everyone else. Explain to each that he or she must . . .

Person 1 . . . speak only while exhaling

Person 2 . . . play *Alphabetical Sequencing Articulation*

Person 3 . . . speak only while inhaling

Person 4 . . . never make eye contact with the subject to whom she is speaking

Person 5 . . . play *Right/Left Brain Counterintuition Discourse* (page 194)

Person 6 . . . end each sentence with ". . . *I'm sorry*." (e.g., Nice to meet you . . . *I'm sorry*; Please pass the gravy . . . *I'm sorry*; Goodnight . . . *I'm sorry*.)

Bonus High

HighLab experimented compounding Right/Left Brain Counter-intuition Discourse with Alphabetical Sequencing Articulation to stunning results. Doing this in public proved especially enlightening—and challenging. The neocortex hangover induced from just two hours of experimentation lasted deep into the following day. A real hard game. But a fun one. Can you do it? Done and done and done!

CYANOBACTERIA

Found everywhere from lakes to oceans, rocks to soil, cyanobacteria have been around the earth for over 2.8 billion years. Sadly, it's only been getting humans high for a couple decades. Marketed as a miracle food in the late 1990s under monikers like Blue-Green Algae Superfood, Spirulina, and Microalgae, manufacturers argue the gross-looking slime improves everything from memory to immune function, digestion to circulation. (Interestingly, it does indeed contain all of the essential amino acids.) In light doses cyanobacteria can also induce a speedy, mildly euphoric physical charge; in heavy doses it will induce headaches, diarrhea, and dizziness.

Get High Now

Companies that sell cyanobacteria recommend 1 to 2 grams a day. HighLab found that while it tastes delicious (we lie—it's repulsive), this amount of algae did not get us high. Extensive and thorough research (e.g., sitting around quaffing algae shakes one Saturday afternoon while watching *Fantasy Island* reruns) revealed that ingesting 4 grams of algae within a single sitting provoked an initial energy rush followed by a tingly, cloudy-head feeling. One HighLab participant said that within a half hour of slamming a Cyanoshake he felt "insect-like: noble, in a Japanese kind of way." If that isn't proof microalgae gets you high, we're not sure what is.

⚠ WARNING: People are different. That's what makes us beautiful. It also makes us react to foods such as cyanobacteria in various ways. Be smart. Be cool. Stay in school! And stick with 2 grams and hope for the best.

TREPANNING (Do Not Do This)

For the *real* heads. Trepanning is the process in which a hole is voluntarily drilled into the crown of one's head with the intention of increasing blood flow to the brain, hence improving memory, sparking creativity, and producing a sense of peaceful well-being. Trepanation is not new; in fact, it is the oldest surgical procedure for which we have evidence, dating back as far as ten thousand years ago. In areas of Europe and Mexico it was considered common. For instance, twenty years ago at a burial ground in France, archaeologists dug up 120 prehistoric skulls dating from 6500 B.C. Forty had been trepanned. Hippocrates wrote specific directions on how to successfully trepan a skull. During the Middle Ages, trepanation was thought to cure various ailments, such as schizophrenia and epilepsy, and it remained popular up through the Renaissance. Some cultures trepanned skulls to cure medical ailments such as seizures, disease, and insanity; others did it for spiritual practices, like removing demons. Today it is used almost exclusively to get high.

Contemporary trepanners claim that the pressure released in the head from the hole causes more blood to reach the brain, leaving the trepanner aware and lucid, in a state they liken to permanent bliss.

Get High Now

Don't drill a hole in your head. Do. Not. Drill. A. Hole. In. Your. Head. If you want to get permanently high, try . . . wait a second, you do not want to get permanently high. Now go do your laundry.

SŌTŌ ZEN FIST

With over 14,700 temples and nearly seven million followers, Sōtō Zen is the largest Zen sect in Japan. Since its inception around the thirteenth century, it's long been considered the Zen discipline of "the people," welcoming everyone from dynastic imperialists to provincial peasants.

Sōtōists practice the form of meditation called Shikantaza, which translates to "nothing but precisely sitting." Exercises in Shikantaza, Sōtōists believe, help to remove the mind and body from consciousness, which allows them to live in a state of pure existence. One Shikantaza exercise is the Zen Fist, which Sōtōists use to help center them in the moment. You can, too. It's easy.

Get High Now

Sit cross-legged on the floor or in a chair. Make a fist of your left hand. Fit your right palm around the fist so that your fingers wrap about halfway around your knuckles. Relax both hands so that you are holding them in form but there is no tension. Drop your hands just below your belly button. Just *do nothing but precisely sit* there for five minutes, longer if you'd like.

Try out the Zen Fist in other meditations, such as Sudarshan Kriya (page 63) or Ten-Stage Breathing (page 238). HighLab members felt the Zen Fist calming for both the mind and body. After a few minutes, some members felt a slight pressure in the spot between their eyes on the forehead (the third eye?). Power of suggestion? Perhaps, but we liked it.

EXPOSURE TO INESCAPABLE PHYSICAL TRAUMA

When placed in situations of extreme stress, humans and other animals respond by flooding their bodies with endorphins. Endorphins are the numbing and pleasure-inducing opiates our pituitary glands secrete when we get excited or experience an orgasm. You've felt the endorphin rush. Now imagine that rush doubled, tripled, quintupled. That's the feeling we get when exposed to inescapable physical trauma.

Bessel A. Van Der Kolk, M.D., argued in a 1989 paper for *Psychiatric Clinics of North America* that this mega-dose of endorphins is the body's mode of self-preservation. When about to be exposed to extreme trauma (say, when you first see that deer jumping out in front of your car), our pituitaries pump us full of endorphins to mute out other senses that could otherwise send us into a painful, death-inducing shock. People who have experienced serious accidents often remember seeing nothing, hearing nothing, *feeling* nothing the few seconds before blacking out. That's the endorphin rush kicking in. This rush is also linked to the ethereal out-of-body experiences that can follow a serious accident, when endorphin levels in our bloodstream can be sky high.

The irony of all this is that the one time in our lives that we feel better than we've ever felt is right before (or after) we are tragically or mortally wounded. Yeah, and you thought God had no sense of humor?

Get High Now

Be "unlucky."

> **Fun Fact:** *Van Der Kolk agues that the mega-endorphin rush is so intense, so utterly euphoric, that it leads some people to reenact and revictimize themselves in traumatic and harmful situations. Among the addicts are masochists, flagellants (see page 172), boxers, and anyone else who purposefully places himself within harm's way to experience a full-body endorphin high.*

AUTO-ELECTROCHARGE EXPANDERS

Our bodies are filled with electric charges: It's how the neurons in our central nervous system communicate with one another, how our body receives messages from our brains. As you would flood the filament of a light bulb with more electricity to make it glow brighter, we can also flood our brain and central nervous system with electrocharges to make us feel higher. This isn't mysticism; it's biology.

An effective way to increase the electricity in your body is through breathing exercises called Auto-Electrocharge Expanders, which not only calm the body but also provide a sense of grounding.

Get High Now

Sit comfortably in a chair or on the floor. Breathe in deeply through your nose, sucking your stomach muscles in towards your spine as far as you can. Try to inhale to a count of about five.

Step One: Hold the thumb of your right hand against your right nostril and breathe out very slowly through your left nostril to a *five* count. Tantrics believe left nostril inhalation calms the nervous system (see Sun & Moon Breath, page 24).

Step Two: Inhale again to a *five* count, holding the right nostril. Once your lungs are completely filled, hold your breath as long as comfortable. While holding your breath, place the forefinger over your left nostril. Exhale to a *five* count through the right nostril. Inhale to a *five* count through the right nostril. This charges your body with energy. Start from the top, exhaling through the left nostril.

Repeat seven times. After a few days, increase to ten times, then more as you feel comfortable. Within a few sessions of Auto-Electrocharge Expanders you should feel a buzz of current flowing through your body and general clarity in your head. That's the increase of electromagnetic pulses in your body, and it feels great.

Note: This exercise is similar to Sun & Moon Breath with the exception that you are alternating nostrils on the inhale and exhale. But, as Mom used to say, what a difference an opposite nostril exhalation does make. Play with both and feel for yourself.

Fun Fact: *When neurons fire in our brains (which happens via electrocharges) they generate an electromagnetic pulse that is detectable in a surrounding electromagnetic field. Some scientists, like Professor Johnjoe McFadden at the University of Surrey in the U.K., argue that this electromagnetic field could actually be related to our consciousness, and that our thoughts float around our brain much the same way a broadcast signal carries messages to a radio.*

THALASSOTHERAPY ☺

We have in our blood a ratio of salt that is almost identical to that of the sea. That's because we are tied to the sea. It's where we evolved from, and to where many of us are constantly trying to return. It's no coincidence 60 percent of the world's population lives in coastal areas. Ask any surfer, sailor, or swimmer what draws him day after day, year after year, to be by and/or within the sea. It is not only a spiritual pull; it's a *chemical* and *biological* need.

Seawater detoxifies the body by leaching out toxins and replenishing our cells with magnesium, potassium, calcium, and more—all minerals that occur in almost identical percentages in seawater as they do in human blood. This is not a coincidence but a reminder of our collective natural history. It feels good to swim in the ocean, because when we do we are going back to our origins.

Thalassotherapy is the practice of bathing in seawater. Though people have been using seawater for medicinal purposes for thousands of years, Thalassotherapy spa treatments didn't fully catch on in Europe until the 1800s. They have recently had a resurgence throughout Italy, Portugal, Morocco, and other countries around the Mediterranean. Many spas in urban areas of the United States now offer some kind of Thalassotherapy.

Get High Now

Thalassotherapy treatments can run about $100 to $200 per session. But if you live along the coast, even in a cold-water climate, consider the amount of a single Thalassotherapy session costs about as much as a wetsuit, which will keep you warm while still giving your skin ample exposure to seawater.

Go to the beach. Welcome yourself into the wide arms of Great Mother Ocean. Some members of HighLab practice this version of Thalassotherapy almost every day of our lives. We know it as a full body/mind high, a spiritual and chemical tonic that lasts throughout the day to which nothing else can compare. Nothing. Go see what you're missing. Go home.

BIOFEEDBACK

Biofeedback works like this: A patient rigs herself up with machines that gauge her bodily functions like heart rate, blood pressure, muscle tension, and brain-wave activity. She watches on a computer as these machines provide live readouts of her body's actions. By monitoring and becoming aware of these immediate conditions, the patient can then use her consciousness to provoke desired changes within her body. She can *think* herself into a different physical state. For instance, if she is suffering from insomnia, she may hook herself up to an electrocardiogram (EKG) and *think* her heart beats slower; her mind becomes calmer, her body lulls into a relaxed sleep state. Or a phobic may monitor her brainwaves while placing herself in an environment in which she has an irrational fear, using the readouts on the biofeedback machine as an anchor to reality for her mind. Doing this, she can eventually overcome her phobia. There are numerous possibilities.

Scientists cannot pinpoint how exactly biofeedback works; all they know is it *does*. And why shouldn't it? If the mind can make us sick, as it does with hypochondriacs, it can surely make us well (see Psychoneuroimmunology, page 42). Numerous scientific studies prove biofeedback's effectiveness in treating alcoholism, chronic pain, epilepsy, insomnia, and various other disorders. It is especially effective in curing urinary incontinence (i.e., wetting one's britches), which affects about 15 million Americans. Based on studies that show a 94 percent reduction in symptoms, the U.S. Department of Health and Human Services in 1996 began recommending biofeedback specifically for this condition. Biofeedback has also proven to help people increase blood flow throughout their bodies, and as such has been used to aid in the symptoms of Raynaud's disease—a disorder in which arteries become constricted, causing areas such as the toes, fingers, nose, and other extremities to turn white or blue.

Fun Fact: *In the 1980s, an associate professor of medicine at the Harvard Medical School, Herbert Benson, used biofeedback machines to record Buddhist monks in the Himalayan Mountains who could, on demand, raise the temperatures of their fingers and toes 17 degrees! Benson led similar studies in 2002, in which bare-chested monks in 40-degree rooms dried cold, wet sheets within an hour, all with their body heat—and all through the power of thinking.*

Get High Now

There are a number of do-it-yourself biofeedback machines available online. HighLab cannot vouch for their efficacy, as we have not used them. But consider any machine that can objectively provide you with information about your bodily conditions as useful. For those serious high-seekers (or those with real problems, the two perhaps not being mutually exclusive), we suggest booking a few sessions with a certified biofeedback specialist.

Biofeedback enables you to hone your conscious ability to affect your physical state to not only make you feel healthy, but dare we say high??? Let's *think* about that!

Funner Fact: *Photoplethysmograph. Electroencephalograph. Hemoencephalography. These are just some of the cool names for the machines used in biofeedback. Reason enough to check it out.*

MUCUNA PRURIENS

The seed pods of this tropical legume tree are six inches long, slightly curved, covered in a thick coat of hair, and have been used for centuries as, guess what, a way for men to induce six-inch long, slightly curved, hair-covered "seed pods" (a.k.a. boners). The magic is in the Mucuna pruriens' high levels of levodopa (L-DOPA), which boosts dopamine in the body. Dopamine, as you should know by now, is the feel-good neurotransmitter and hormone associated with activities such as eating good food and having sex. It also increases arousal and motor activity and aids in our ability to stay in and delve deeper into vivid Lucid Dreams (see page 99).

Get High Now

Mucuna pruriens can be found at most health-food and fitness stores. Different brands offer different dosages for different reasons. The standard dosage our flaccid brothers of Southeast Asia use is about a half ounce. We stuck with that. HighLab will not comment on the Mucuna's aphrodisiac qualities, but will say that this legume did little to boost lucid dream states. Perhaps we didn't take enough; perhaps the fact that we were all sleep deprived (see page 59) had something to do with it. Try it for yourself.

SELF-IMPOSED INVOLUNTARY ABDUCTION ♊

Some S&M tweakers get a high out of being taken some place against their will and abused, so much so that cities like New York and San Francisco now offer forms of "abduction services." HighLab finds this practice offensive, not because we believe people shouldn't have the liberty to get perverted, but because some folks actually *pay* to have it done.

The thrill of being taken immediately out of context, somewhere beyond your comfort area will charge you with a primitive, survivalist high—one seldom experienced in our meticulously proscribed, controlled society. Some people experience a feeling of rebirth after the abduction; others experience gonorrhea. Be careful.

Get High Now

Prearrange for a friend or group to abduct you at some time in the next month. Do not establish activities, locations, time, or any other details. The less you know about the abduction, the better. As part of the arrangement, have them drop you somewhere you have never been, for an undetermined amount of time, and leave you. . . .

Chapter Four:

CALMING HIGHS

MUD SLEEP INDUCTION

Agrypniaphobics go to bed with every intention of falling asleep, but then worry that they might not be able to sleep, a worry that gets them nervous, a nervousness that makes them toss and turn, a tossing-and-turning that makes them unable to lie still, unable to close their eyes, unable to sleep, because they are worried, because they are nervous, because they toss and turn. Because they are agrypniaphobics.

If this were a book about getting high *with* drugs, we would suggest agrypniaphobics dose heavily on Demerol, Vicodin, Valium, sleeping pills, or 4 ounces of Robitussin (known on the streets of San Francisco as "Dr. Mom"). But no such luck. So what's a non-drug-taking agrypniaphobic to do? Get muddy, buddy.

Mud Sleep Induction is a popular exercise hypnotists use when they are trying to relax restless patients into a sleep state. Though its effectiveness is unproven for agrypniaphobics, High-Lab found it a great way to calm down before sleeping at night.

Get High Now

Lay down on a bed or a couch. Shut your eyes about halfway. Imagine yourself sitting on the sand of a beach. You are at the water's edge. Dig your feet into the wet sand. It is warm. It feels good. Now dig your legs in a little. Imagine using your hands to cover your legs. The weight of the sand is comforting, like a blanket. Lean back. Slowly take the wet, warm sand and cover yourself up to your waist. Feel the weight of the sand. Now cover your stomach, then the chest. Dig your hands and arms into the sand. Feel it on your limbs, your body. Your feet sink a bit deeper, then your legs. Your body is covered in sand, you feel its heavy weight all around you. You can't move, but you don't want to anyway; the warmth of the sand is calm and comforting. The sand is growing heavier, you sink in a bit more. You close your eyes. You sink so deep. Now sleep.

HOPS

You think it's just the alcohol in beer that gets you feelin' free and easy? Well, it is. But give hops some props. If taken on their own, the female flowers of the hop plant can induce a mild, semi-stoned high. This is caused by the high amounts of methylbutanal, a natural alcohol that, when ingested, works as a sedative on our central nervous system. Wonder why your friends want to go home after drinking two hoppy microbrews? Blame the methylbutanal, which has a side effect of sleepiness.

Since the Jews first used them in Babylon as far back as 400 B.C., hops have been added to beer to instill bitterness and floral aromas to the otherwise sweet taste of plain beer malt. The alpha acids in hops also help protect beer against unwanted bacteria and reduce the amount of unwanted organisms during fermentation.

Get High Now

Hops are legal everywhere and can be acquired at beer supply and natural food grocery stores. Two members of HighLab boiled about 4 grams of hops, extracted the tea, and drank it one Tuesday afternoon. (This is what freelance advertising art directors do in between contracts. Art school students: You've been warned!) Both fellows experienced a general feeling of relaxation and well-being, as well as a slight alcohol-like buzz—almost exactly the same feeling as drinking a beer or two, but without all the fuss with bottle openers.

⚠ WARNING: Animals that ingested large quantities of hops were prone to seizures, skittishness, and other maladies. Some people may be allergic to hops. We suggest before trying them, rub a small amount on a sensitive part of your skin—backside of elbow, or backside of wrist—and monitor for a reaction.

AMYGDALA EXCERCISALA

Lift the forefinger of your right hand up and down twice. Do it now. Good. What has just happened is that your brain has given your body a mental command to commit a physical action. Yeah, it's like magic. Actually, it's not. We use our brains to do menial physical tasks tens of thousands of times a day.

Our brains control our external movements in the world. We know that. But what most of us don't realize is that our brains can also control our *internal movements*, how we feel inside, how we react, our moods, and even our health. Our brains can make us high (see Psychoneuroimmunology, page 42). All we have to do are some simple Amygdala Excercisalas.

The amygdalae are nut-sized reservoirs of neurons located in the middle of the left and right hemispheres of the brain that control some aspects of emotion and memory. By focusing mental energy on the two amygdalae, some believe we can provoke the neurochemical activity into the frontal lobes, which contain most of the dopamine-sensitive neurons. Stimulating this area makes us feel good, and can also spark creativity and intelligence. Yes. Sounds too hippy-dippy to bother with, eh? Tell that to the numerous MRI and PET technicians who recorded considerable electrochemical change in the brain of people who practiced Amygdala Excercisalas.

Researcher T. D. A. Lingo (yes, that's his real name) at the Dormant Brain Research and Development Laboratory (yes, that's its real name) in Blackhawk, Colorado, conducted a study from 1957 to 1993 on the effectiveness of self-stimulating the amygdalae. Part of the study involved 309 students practicing some of the amygdala exercises on the following pages. Lingo believed that concentrating on moving the amygdala forward—he called it "clicking"—participants could stimulate their frontal lobes and thus increase their consciousness and receptiveness to spiritual states. They could get high. Lingo found the vast majority of subjects who took part in the study experienced a "transcendent phenomenon" and as a result reported an increase of intelligence, creativity, and positive emotions.

Get High Now

Look closely at the illustration of the amygdalae. Notice how they are located just below the temples toward the ears, about an inch from the back corners of the eyes. Concentrate on them: one on the right hemisphere, the other on the left. Simply *thinking* about "clicking" your amygdala works. Try it. When you are ready, try a few of the more advanced techniques that follow. What's wild is that after a couple minutes a few HighLab members who tried this really *felt* it work. Yes, up there in our brains. It feels good and, if anything, it beats lifting your forefinger up and down.

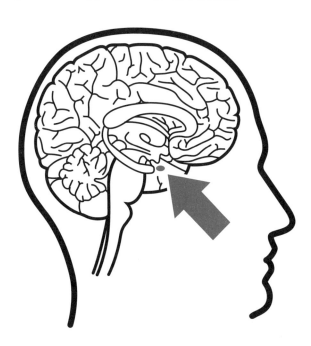

Dog Nose Clicking

Dogs rely on instincts and a keen sense of smell—both things that are heavily influenced by their cute little puppy amygdalae. When dogs smell something good, their amygdalae react by "clicking forward," sending impulses to glands that activate good-feeling neurotransmitters like dopamine. Dogs relate the good-smelling thing with *feeling* good and thus will seek this smell out in the future. Alternately, when dogs smell something bad their amygdalae send negative messages to their brains, making them want to get away from the smell—their amygdalae "click backwards." Humans process smells in the same way dogs do.

Get High Now

Open up your fridge. Grab some old yogurt, cottage cheese, milk—something now rotten that you've forgotten to throw out. Smell it. That pukey reaction you just had? It's the feeling of your amygdalae clicking backwards. That's your brain telling you to get away. You develop this negative association—this clicking backwards of the amygdalae—with things you should avoid.

Now grab a fresh orange or a bottle of Chartreuse. Smell it. It smells good. The smell gives you pleasure. That's the feeling of your amygdalae clicking forward. It's your brain's way of telling you what's in front of you is OK to get close to, to be near, eat, or rub on your skin. This is how humans evolved, by being able to process the messages sent by amygdalae to help us to safely judge our surroundings. It's also how we developed our advanced reasoning skills and the ability to properly choose between what is good and bad for us.

Bonus High

Imagine a long feather slowly and softly falling on top of your head. Take a deep breath. Imagine the feather sinking into your head and lightly tickling the amygdalae. Feel your thoughts moving forward, feel "the click." Do this for at least two minutes. Two HighLab members actually reported *feeling* this click, claiming it to be at first disarming then comforting. Both members said they felt great for hours after. You can, too. Do it. Tickle, tickle!

SLOW WORDS

Light is not just something we see, it is also "stuff," a bunch of photons, vibrating at different speeds. The speed at which light vibrates is known as its "wavelength." The human eye can only see light when it vibrates at a wavelength of about 400 to 700 nanometers (one nanometer = a billionth of a meter). Light at this speed is first "sensed" by our eyes then "perceived" into recognizable patterns. These patterns are how we form our perception of the world around us (for a related audio high see Risset Rhythm, page 168).

Throughout the day, we correctly sense and perceive millions of images. In adult life, most of images are easy and we understand them instantly. We've had a lot of practice. However, complicated light formations that our brains are not attuned to process, such as illusions, may be instantly "sensed" but can take longer for our brains to "perceive"—to process into something we can recognize and understand. Slow Words is one such illusion.

Get High Now

Look at the Slow Words pattern. Most people will see a random assortment of blobs. Your eyes "sense" the objects, but you "perceive" them as unrecognizable forms.

Continue staring at them. Don't try to see anything, don't try to understand them, just stare. Eventually, you will begin to "perceive" the objects as two different words. It takes some people a few moments, others minutes, others still longer. Once you figure out the words, you will be able to quickly recognize them the next time you see them. That's because you've stored a memory of the objects, and instead of going through the process of trying to "perceive" them again, all your brain need do is tap that memory for an answer.

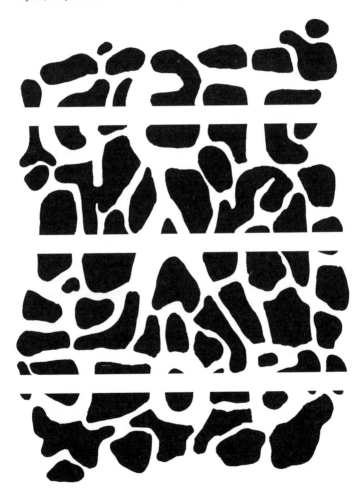

CATNIP

Catnip is to the feline what malt liquor is to the urban hobo: delicious and fortifying . . . and a convenient way to get quickly obliterated. Catnip grows all over, from North America to Africa, Asia to Europe. Traditionally, it has been used as everything from an insect repellent (it's more effective than DEET) to a cure for toothaches, a spice, and, of course, as crack for cats. Untraditionally, catnip can be used as a mild psychotropic and relaxant for humans.

The stoning goodness in catnip is its nepetalactones, an organic compound that is also found in certain ants throughout California, and the reason Native Americans were drawn to eating live ants as a means to get high (see Ants, page 22).

Get High Now

Fresh catnip is available at most pet stores. Take about 3 grams and steep it in a pot for about five minutes. Serve any way you like. Four members of HighLab split a large pot of catnip (we penned its street name "Fancy Feast" and served it chilled in cognac glasses with one teaspoon honey and a maraschino cherry). The effects were subtle but relaxing and soothing, like the cedarwood scents in the dangerously erotic men's cologne, Drakkar Noir.

BLIND SPOTS

Most of us think vision is a straight-lined path from the eyes to cognition. Fact is, all visual input makes a stop-off in the brain for "processing" before we "understand" what it is we are looking at. While processing, the brain has to constantly assume details in order to keep up with the constant flow of visual data. (See Chronosynclastic Infundibulum, page 161; Vomit Vectors, page 161; and Risset Rhythm, page 168.) When the eyes can offer only scant details on an object (in dark environments, for instance) the brain has to make especially broad assumptions. It starts filling in the visual blanks with whatever it considers *should* go there. That's right, the brain does what any self-respecting lawyer does when faced with inadequate evidence: it makes stuff up.

$$+ \qquad\qquad \bullet$$

And the brain does this *all the time*. Though it may seem like it, the eye does not provide us with a perfect, unhindered field of vision. There are obstacles, blind spots on the eye itself that we can't see past. We don't see these obstacles because the brain fills in these blanks, assuming similar colors, shades, and textures it takes from the surrounding field of vision. In this, *every single thing* we look at is partially "imagined" by the brain, a quasi-illusion of the world patched up with visual assumptions.

Let's go deeper into this for a moment. Think of the eye as a windshield, with our brains in the passenger seat. Our brains really want an unhindered field of vision, a clear windshield, but there's that pesky rear-view mirror in the way. The rear-view mirror represents the eye's optic nerve head, which collects signals from the eye and scoots them back to the brain. Where the head of this optic nerve connects to the eye, usually in the middle (just like the rear-view mirror), no signals can be sent to the brain—that is, we cannot *see* in this area. The brain fills this optic nerve head blind spot with whatever visual data is around it; the brain piecemeals what it *thinks* should go there. It's as if the brain is putting matching "windshield" wallpaper over the rear-view mirror so it can pretend to get a totally clear view of what's ahead.

Get High Now

Put your hand over your left eye. Hold the + sign (see previous page) at around arm's length. You'll notice the circle next to the +, but don't look at it. Keep your attention on the +. Slowly bring the book closer. Stare at the +. When you have the page at about a foot distance, you'll suddenly notice the • has disappeared. This is where the optic nerve head is; this is your blind spot. It's a surprisingly huge area that most people never realize exists.

COLORED NOISE ⑨

Noise annoys. It has also been linked to heart disease, hypertension, immune deficiency, the really scary-sounding *presbycusis* (gradual hearing loss due to aging), and dozens of other ailments. In 1978, the U.S. Environmental Protection Agency showed a high rate of birth defects among mothers who were exposed to elevated levels of environmental noise on a regular basis. Later studies confirmed these findings. In a 2000 study by the Toronto Public Health Department, scientists found prolonged exposure to environmental noise can also cause biochemical changes in the body that affect the normal regulation of growth hormones. No wonder members of speed metal bands are so short.

Though noise is defined as a random signal, it is often classified into areas: environmental noise, industrial noise, occupational noise, etc. It is also classified into "colors." Engineers originally developed "colored" noises to use as guides for electric, acoustic, and audio equipment experiments. Each noise was named after the color it most closely resembled in frequency. (Different colors vibrate at a different frequencies, which is how the human eye distinguishes them. See Chromotherapy, page 76.) In the early 1970s, colored noises were used to test for extrasensory perception.

Dr. Charles Honorton, among other parapsychologists, believed white and pink noise played through headphones could mute out the senses and make a person more amenable to subconscious thought. In Ganzfeld Anomalous Information Transfer experiments (page 50), extended exposure to white or pink noise was often successful in inducing in subjects hypnagogia and other altered states of consciousness. At a minimum, a few minutes of white or pink noise placed people into a deep state of meditation.

Colored noise highs are easy—all you do to turn on is turn it up.

Get High Now

Noise affects people differently. Though the Ganzfeld experiment suggests white or pink noise, any noise can theoretically be used to mute out thoughts and place you into a deeper, more introspective state. Different colored noises all have a distinct tactile feel about them; some, like brown noise, feel warm and comforting, while others, like violet noise, are cold and agitating. Grab some headphones, go to Gethighnow.com, test a few out, and pick one you like. Listen to your color while sitting or lying down comfortably with your eyes closed for at least five minutes. Noise is Novocaine for the brain.

White Noise

This is a flat-spectrum noise, which makes it equally powerful in any given bandwidth. HighLab found this noise full-bodied, with a zesty finish.

Pink Noise

This is a softer version of white noise, offering a muted ashiness and a carmellowy head-feel.

Brown Noise

Our favorite. Sumptuous, *doux* overtones with robust body. Intoxicating. Brown noise is known as the "random walk" or "drunkard's walk." It gets its name not from the color, but Brownian motion, the seemingly random movement of particles first described by Scottish botanist Robert Brown (1773–1853).

Violet Noise

This noise changes its value as inputs change, increasing 6 decibels per octave. It boasts a metallic, thin quality with a pointed body. Not for the weak.

DING BOW STANCE

You know that old lady in the polyester jogging suit with a full-face sun visor who is up at 6 A.M. every morning in the same corner of the park looking like she's slo-mo poppin'? Well, she isn't rehearsing moves for the upcoming Cool Kids show—she's enriching her health, prolonging her life, and getting a full-body high. She's practicing Tai Chi. Hundreds of millions of people around the world do the same everyday. You will soon make it hundreds of millions plus one.

Tai Chi, which translates to the awesome-sounding "supreme ultimate fist," originated in China in the early 1800s. Simply put, it is an amalgam of martial-arts postures housed in five different family styles: Wu/Hao, Chen, Yang, Wu, and Sun. The Yang Style is the most widely practiced today and recognized for its poetic and soulful movements. The below is just one of 24 stances that constitute a simple Tai Chi morning routine.

Get High Now

Position One: Stand on even ground, indoors or out. Put your heels together with your toes turning out at 45 degrees (about two and ten o'clock). Look down as you bend, lowering yourself until just the tips of your knees cover your toes. Hang your arms loosely at your sides. Your hands should lightly touch your thighs. Find your balance, keeping your torso straight. Lift your head so that you are looking straight ahead. Close your eyes and stand there for about 10 seconds. Become the form.

Position Two: When ready, step your left foot out about 12 inches at the same 45-degree angle in which it is already pointed. Lightly

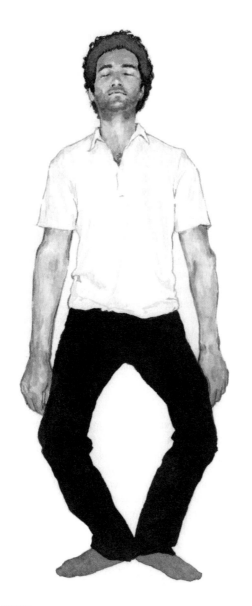

tap the toe to the ground while keeping your left knee bent. There should be no tension in your left leg. Open your eyes and look down to make sure the left toes are about in line with your left shoulder. Once set, close your eyes. Hold this position for a few seconds, then bring the left foot back to Position One. Follow the same steps with your right foot. Repeat on each side ten times.

HighLab found this posture a little awkward in the beginning. After a few rounds it gets easier, and by the end the exercise provides a feeling of centeredness. As for the fabulously toned butt cheeks the stance also promotes, we need only say: "Ding Wow!"

NEGATIVE AFTERIMAGES

A negative afterimage is an optical high in which the color of an object appears in its opposite color for a few moments after you look away from it.

In your eye are little cells called photoreceptors, which communicate with the retina to help you to see. If you stare at a certain image long enough, these photoreceptors will grow tired and stop responding with the retina. The *active* photoreceptors around the *bored* photoreceptors will then take over and send signals to the retina. But these active photoreceptors send the wrong signals—swapping the original color of the image for its opposite. Yes, our eyes work in some counterintuitive and baffling ways. (See Positive Afterimages, page 72, for more ocular fun!)

Get High Now

Go to Gethighnow.com and stare at the image for a minimum of one minute. When you are done, look at a white wall or plain sheet of paper. What you will see is an afterimage with the colors on the opposite end of the color spectrum from those you were staring at.

HEMISPHERIC SYNCHRONIZATION (Hemi-Sync)

This audio high was developed in the 1970s by Robert Monroe, an advertising executive who had an out-of-body experience one November night in 1958. In the previous month Monroe had experimented with "sleep-learning," in which he played an audio loop during sleeping hours to provoke lucid dreams and stir his subconscious. The past few nights Monroe had experienced very strange, visceral sensations in his body during dreams, feelings of weightlessness, tingling, and numbness in his fingers. Then, one night in November, he pressed *PLAY* on the tape loop, closed his eyes, and it started: the body vibrations, numb limbs, bright light inches from his face. Soon after he described floating above his own body. Monroe would spend the rest of his life trying—and ultimately succeeding—to duplicate the experience. As well as authoring books and holding workshops, Monroe developed audio tapes using a technique called *Hemispheric Synchronization*, which he claimed could help induce out-of-body experiences.

Hemi-Sync doesn't lull listeners into a state of meditation with spacey soft rock or harp-and-flute solos, it causes an *actual* physiological change, rewiring the space between the hemispheres of our brains to induce one of the oddest and most confusing audio hallucinations most people will ever experience. It works under the same premise as Binaural Beats (see page 48 for an explanation). Monroe suggested Hemi-Sync not only opens doors to altered states of consciousness, but also boosts health, spiritual, and physical fitness.

fMRIs show Hemi-Sync actually *does* work, successfully training the brain into the same rhythm. Whether it sends us out-of-body is entirely subjective, but hey, it's worth giving it a go.

Fun Fact: *The same way sound waves can physically alter the world around us—rumbling walls and shattering glass— they can also entrain our minds and bodies. This is how Binaural Beats, Hemi-Sync, and other audio therapies work. Each adjusts our brainwaves to a specific speed that will slow other processes like breathing and heart rate to a meditative state. Entrainment is why we can feel music—the music is not only mentally or psychologically affecting us, it is altering the beat of our body, literally moving us.*

Get High Now

In 1974, Monroe founded the cultish-sounding Monroe Institute, an "organization dedicated to providing a positive environment for the continuing transformation of human consciousness." Since his death in 1995, Monroe's followers have expanded the Monroe empire to include all manner of Hemi-Sync products, including CDs that can purportedly help listeners cure cancer and even communicate with animals. The curious can check these products out via the Monroe Institute Web site. A selection produced by the Monroe Institute can also be downloaded on iTunes. HighLab tried out "Convergence," and although we unfortunately did not experience the out-of-body awesomeness Monroe reported in his trials, two members did recall moments of mild hypnosis with weird visions.

Funner Fact: *Robert Monroe is credited with coining the term "out-of-body experience."*

QIGONG DIAPHRAGMATIC BREATH

Translating roughly to "cosmic breath," *Qigong* is a collection of therapeutic breathing, movement, and meditation techniques practiced by hundreds of millions of Chinese. Its roots trace back over four thousand years.

For some Qigongers, this more spiritual and mystical step-child of Tai Chi is used to cleanse and maintain strong health in body and mind; others use it to energize. In studies conducted in 2006 by the *Journal of Alternative and Complementary Medicine*, Qigong was proven to reduce pulse rate and blood pressure, and increase metabolism—all good things. In fact, Qigong has become so popular that it has become a standard medical practice in China and is promoted in China's National Health Plan.

The most important aspect of any Chinese meditation, especially "cosmic breath," is the way in which we inhale and exhale air. Qigong exercises promotes drawing air deep into the lungs so that the stomach extends, not the chest. This kind of *diaphragmatic* breathing is shared by animals and babies. Watch them breathe sometime and you will see that each inhales deeply, expanding his stomach with air. Humans lose this innate, natural *diaphragmatic* breathing, according to some, as we begin to walk on two feet, exposing our stomach and lungs vertically instead of horizontally. Qigong Diaphragmatic Breath re-teaches us this technique, and in the process floods the body with oxygen, relaxes the autonomic nervous system, and can also prepare the body and mind for deep meditation. It feels great.

Get High Now

Sit comfortably on the floor or in a chair. Loosen your belt or pants if they are tight, or, better, change into loose clothes. Place one hand on your stomach and the other on your chest. Purse your lips, inhaling through them slowly to a count of about seven. (It's fine to breathe through your nose as you inhale.) Feel your stomach extend. If you feel your chest expand with each inhale, keep practicing until you feel only your stomach extend.

Exhale slowly through your pursed lips, for a count of about seven or longer if you can. Repeat about thirty times, or until you feel clearheaded (e.g., mildly and wonderfully high). With enough practice you will be able to breathe this way any time you feel stressed out, nervous, or if you just want to feel good. Some HighLab members swear ten minutes of Qigong Diaphragmatic Breathing will cure any headache, tension, and even the most vicious hangover. Give it a Qi-go.

RUSSIAN REINDEER THAT HAVE JUST INGESTED URINE AND EATEN AMANITA MUSCARIA MUSHROOMS

The Chukchi tribe of Siberia feed their reindeer human urine. They believe the urine improves the reindeer's endurance. The reindeer love it, perhaps not only for the taste but because the urine gets them drunk. When the Chukchi relieve themselves, the reindeer fight over who gets to munch the yellow snow. This, my friends, is all true.

Beyond being prodigious urinators, the Chukchi are also trippers who frequently munch on the psychotropic *Amanita muscaria* mushroom. They seek out this magic mushroom in the wilds of the tundra, and also seek out the animals that have just ingested it. Whenever the Chukchi see a reindeer listening to colors, smelling lights, or generally acting like a stoned hippy in the park, they quickly slaughter the animal and eat its flesh. The psychoactive properties of the *Amanita muscaria* mushroom transfer from the animal blood into the Chukchis, leaving the Chukchis with not only full bellies of delicious fresh reindeer meat, but with full minds of cosmic, psychedelic visions.

Now check this out: The Chukchi then save *their* hallucinogenic-infused urine (the byproduct of the hallucinogenic-infused reindeer meat they just ate) so that they can later drink it or share it with others in the tribe to get high *again*. This is perhaps the truest form of psychedelic recycling (or shall we say "repsychling").

Get High Now

Go to Siberia. Befriend a Chukchi. (Bring mouthwash.)

CO-PARTNERED MENTAL/ORAL CHAKRA STIMULATION

For those uninitiated to the more cosmic sides of yoga, chakras are "energy centers" that run from the top of the head down to the tip of the spine: There is the *Sahasrara* (top of head), the *Ajna* (eyebrow area), *Vishuddha* (throat), *Anahata* (heart), *Manipura* (navel), *Swadhisthana* (pelvic area), and *Muladhara* (coccyx point at the tip of the spine). Many forms of meditation engage the chakras to energize, relax, and bring enlightenment and peace to your mind and body. We engage them to get high.

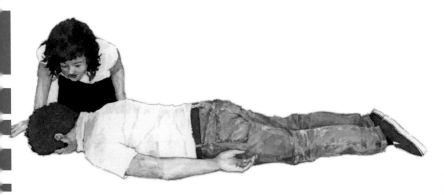

Get High Now

A "receiver" lies on the floor with his stomach down, head to the side. He takes three deep breaths. Once relaxed, a "chanter" approaches, bending down to place her mouth at the top of the receiver's head, the *Sahasrara* chakra point. The chanter inhales, then softly chants *Om* as she exhales to a count of about *ten*, simultaneously concentrating all her mental energy on the *Sahasrara* area. She repeats this process a total of three times for each chakra down the spine.

HighLab participants reported a "levitational" feeling and general good vibe hours after the exercise.

MECHANICAL/MEDICINAL PHOSPHENE INDUCTION: INTERGALACTIC & TRANSCRANIAL MAGNETIC STIMULATION

Intense phosphene highs can be induced by sending electricity through the brain in the form of Transcranial Magnetic Stimulation (TMS) (page 178). Used to treat patients suffering from strokes, Parkinson's disease, tinnitus, and other ailments, TMS promotes an increase of endorphins, serotonin, and dopamine in the body . . . in other words, it gets you really high. The problem—if you can call it that—is that TMS can only be applied by professionals to patients. And it sometimes produces seizures. And it's expensive. For these reasons, HighLab does not recommend TMS.

However, we *do* recommend Intergalactic Phosphene Stimulation. This occurs when reentering the earth's atmosphere after being exposed to intergalactic radiation. Astronauts regularly experience mind-blowing phosphene highs at moments of reentry, to the point that they feel they are hallucinating or going cuckoo. Of the 59 astronauts surveyed by NASA and the ESA (European Space Agency), 47 reported some phosphene illusions during spaceflight. Most recalled bright white flashes in elongated shapes that appeared to be moving either in and out, side to side, or diagonally, but, strangely never in vertical formations.

Get High Now

According to Virgin Galactic, space tourism is right around the corner. In the meantime, impatient intergalactic phosphene high seekers can pay the Russian government upwards of $20 million, train, and join a spaceflight as a civilian crewmember. Accompany the cosmonaut crew into space. Dig the reentry.

PERIPHERAL DRIFT

Academic tenure rules. Long naps in the afternoon; a council of assistants to correct class papers; months-long sabbaticals to "work on the novel." And tons of eye-blinking. That is, if you are *le professeur* Jocelyn Faubert, Ph.D. (*Psychophysique de la vision*) at the Université de Montréal. He and researcher Andrew Herbert spent Canadian taxpayer dollars researching how "circularly repeating patches containing sawtooth luminance gradients produce a sensation of motion when viewed in the periphery." Translation: how to get high from looking at a circle while blinking your eyes real quick.

Faubert found that when blinking our eyes within view of gradated dark and light sections, the eye will lose its place then have to refocus; the brain will then have trouble processing the signals from the eyes, or "differing latencies in the processing of luminance." The result is a perceived motion within a stationary illustration, or, a head-tripping buzz.

Get High Now

Look just slightly to the side of the image. The image should move. Now blink your eyes as quickly as possible. Do not look at the image; keep it in your peripheral vision. Watch it move. When it does, hoist your fist and give three cheers for academia.

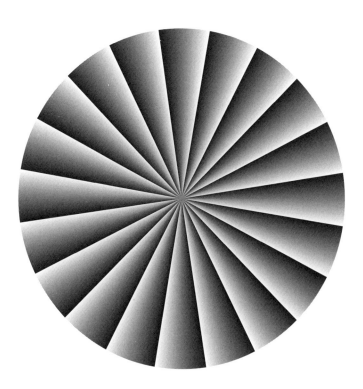

PASSION FLOWER

The name "passion flower" (from the *Passiflora* genus, which contains over 500 species of plants) comes from the Christian belief that the red petals of this flower represent the Passion of Jesus Christ during the crucifixion. Other Christians see the petals as resembling the bloody crown of thorns Jesus wore on the cross. Still others argue the petals symbolize Jesus's apostles. Why so much blood and pain attributed to this innocent little flower? What were these Christians thinking? They weren't— they were too busy getting hammered from ingesting the petals of this psychedelic plant.

Passion flower, or *Passiflora incarnata* if you must, contains three potentially psychoactive chemicals: harmala alkaloids, apigenine, and C-glycosyfavones. It is unclear which of these chemicals account for the flower's effects, however researchers *did* find that harmala alkaloids in many species are effective antidepressants. Further, harmala alkaloids reduce the breakdown in the human digestive system of dimethyltryptamine (DMT), a potent psychedelic produced by plants as well as the human body. Reducing the breakdown in the digestive system will make DMT more potent. But is it enough to get us high? The indigenous people of upper South America perhaps think so. They use passion flower along with various other plants to make *ayahuasca*, the cripplingly hallucinogenic drink that has been a part of sacred ceremonies around the Amazon for over 2,500 years.

Get High Now

In Europe, passion flower has been used for centuries to calm the mind and induce sleep. Most prepare tea with about 3 grams of passion flower petals and stems in a pot, bring the mixture to a boil for about 15 minutes, let it steep, then extract the tea. (Note: The roots and stems contain much higher concentrations of harmala alkaloids than do the petals.) The effects are reported to be mild but pleasurable. In the right quantities passion flower tea allegedly induces a slight distortion of colors and sleepiness. Try a cup before bed and see what happens.

ASTRAL PROJECTION

This is the act of channeling our "spiritual body," that gossamer thing that floats in the higher planes above us laughing with its perfect teeth and combing its long white hair as we pick gum from our shoes on the grubby sidewalks of earth.

For millennia, cultures around the world have been trying to reach the astral plane through chants, trance, drugs, whatever. The Greeks considered getting astral the highest state of human consciousness, naming it *ekstasis*—"to stand outside of oneself"—a state they described as indescribably joyful. It is from the Greek *ekstasis* that the English word "ecstasy" is derived.

We allegedly inhabit the astral body in near-death or out-of-body experiences, and it is the same body that floats you away when you die and go to heaven—or hell, if you are Ronnie James Dio or Bryant Gumbel. Ten percent of the U.S. population claims to have had an out-of-body experience, that is, tripped the astral plane.

Get High Now

The final moments of dying are alleged to be the most tried-and-true way to enter the astral plane, but then, you'd be dead, and worse, you won't be around to purchase the sequel, *Get High Now II: How to Get Ripped with Drugs and Alcohol*. Olde time psychic Hereward Carrington (1880–1959) developed a number of ways to get astral in his crazy 1929 book, *The Projection of the Astral Body*. Thousands of other books have followed in the past eighty years, all with their own methods.

The techniques are varied and often complicated, but all share the same general premise: To get astral we need simply *will* our consciousness from our bodies into the outside world, usually during states of deep meditation or sleep. Next time you are in bed preparing for sleep, *think* yourself outside your body. That's it. It takes practice, astral projectors say, but everyone can do it.

> **Fun Fact:** *Oh yes, astral projection is pretty cosmic stuff. But consider that your brain already emits an electromagnetic field that is detectable outside your head—a scientific fact. If our consciousness is already outside our bodies, is it so much of a stretch to believe we can shift it to other rooms? Astral projectors don't think so; they practice shifting themselves not only around the house, but to other towns, countries, even other planets! To have sex with aliens! (No joke. There are astral projection workshops on how to do just that, and so much more. Hot!)*

TEN-STAGE BREATHING

A HighLab original! This exercise was derived from a three-stage breathing exercise copped from a 1970s meditation book. The effects of three-stage breathing were too mild for us to fully qualify as a "high," so two HighLab members began lengthening the prescribed breath counts to ten. These effects were instant and revelatory. Within a few cycles of Ten-Stage Breathing all HighLab members experienced a feeling of extreme serenity and calmness.

Get High Now

Sit comfortably in a chair. Keep your eyes opened or closed, whichever is most comfortable. Make sure that your back is supported by a back rest, and that it is fully relaxed. Breathe in slowly through your nose to the count of *one one-thousand*. Breathe out slowly through your nose, adding a number to the count, *one one-thousand, two one-thousand*. Next, repeat the count you just exhaled—*one one-thousand, two one-thousand*—and with the next exhale add another count, *one one-thousand, two one-thousand, three one-thousand*. Follow this exercise to a count of *ten one-thousand*, then count back down following the same inhale-exhale pattern. Repeat the whole cycle (up and down) three times. Now entering stage left: a wonderfully meditative mind and tingly body—yours.

THE CAFÉ WALL ☺

This New Wave-ish visual high was first recorded in Bristol, England, in 1973 by Dr. Richard Gregory, now emeritus professor of neuropsychology at the University of Bristol. A member of Gregory's lab was on the way to work one day and noticed a pulsating, otherworldly display on the wall of a café. Nothing about the materials or construction of the wall was odd; it was a simple alternating black-and-white tile pattern with rows offset by a half-width, each surrounded by a thin border of grout. Though the materials and the construction were simple, the effect was hypnotic.

The Café Wall works by feeding our brain too much contrasting information at once. Our visual systems are not very precise when perceiving strong contrasts in color, and the strong black-and-white pattern with mortar in the middle on the Café Wall immediately overpowers the brain.

When we look at Café Wall we don't notice the mortar as being separate from the alternating black and white tiles; we instead assume the mortar is a part of whichever tiles are *closest* to our field of vision. Since we think the mortar and the tile it is closest to are one object, our brains must then assume that the tile containing the mortar *must* be larger than the tile *not* containing the mortar. But then when we look at Café Wall, we see that *all* the tiles contain mortar! How can one object be bigger than another if they are all the same size and containing the same edging of mortar? They can't. And the only way our brains can make any logical sense out of these discrepancies is by assuming the tiles themselves aren't all the same size, but incongruous wedges.

OK, this gets even more complicated but stick with it, troopers. So, if the brain assumes the tiles as wedges, the mortar between the tiles then must be making these tiles wedges—this is the only possible solution for how the Café Wall could look as it does. But when we look at Café Wall again we see that the mortar is undoubtedly straight and evenly distributed between tiles. (*What the?!?*) So how then could all these wedges be in this picture? Having no other option to make sense of this conundrum (that a straight line of mortar is making a bunch of obtuse wedges) the brain resolves the problem by assuming the mortar is: a) indeed a straight line but b) that it is tilting at varying degrees through the tiles, either up or down, just slightly. This assumption allows the black-and-white squares to logically be wedges *and* the mortar to be in a straight line. Having no other choice, the brain assumes this. But the brain is wrong. And this is why we see the Café Wall as a series of tilted straight lines separating wedge-shaped tiles.

The above is a theory. Fact is, the verdict is *still* out on exactly why our visual system and brain perceives Café Wall the way it does. Feel free to study up and join in the debate, or do what we do: Forget about all this neurological gibber-jab and just look at it. Just get high.

For similar illusionary highs, see Chronosynclastic Infundibulum (page 161) and Ouchi Goochi (page 190).

Get High Now

Stare at the pattern for a moment. Does the pattern grow distorted and funneled at the tips? Examine it closely and you'll see the alternating black and white lines are actually completely straight and square.

MULBERRY SAP (Do Not Do This)

The white latex sap that accumulates on the unripe fruit and green parts of the mulberry tree is psychotropic. What makes it so is piperidine, an organic compound that is also found in fire-ant toxin, tobacco, poison hemlock, and black pepper, from which it gets its name. Though it is now used in many antipsychotic prescription drugs, piperidine got a rightfully bad reputation in the 1970s as a main ingredient in the manufacture of the debilitating and lethal drug PCP.

Get High Now

In the right doses mulberry sap is hallucinogenic; in wrong doses it induces extreme vomiting, diarrhea, and could kill you. The line between the two is very slim. Don't be an idiot.

However, the ripe mulberry fruit, not only a delectable filling to pies and pastries, contains large amounts of resveratrol, an antibody the tree produces to protect it from fungi and bacteria. In a 2003 study published in *Nature* resveratrol extended the lifespan of yeast, worms, and fruit flies. In a 2006 Italian study, resveratrol extended the life of a fish by over 50 percent. Now, go eat some mature mulberry fruit—and get high off (a long, long) life.

SAMATHA LEVEL DHAMMAKĀYA MEDITATION

According to Thai monk Phramongkolthepmuni, the founder of Dhammakāya school of meditation, the Buddha became enlightened using a particular form of meditation, the name and practice of which was lost for a few thousand years after the Buddha reached final nirvana. Phramongkolthepmuni (say that ten times fast) claimed to have "rediscovered" this meditation in Thailand in 1914, after which he formed the Dhammakāya movement. The movement's Buddha-style meditation is now practiced by over seven million people worldwide. Research at London's King's College and in the *Physiology & Behavior* journal has shown that this meditation significantly reduces anxiety, stress, and depression.

Dhammakāya meditation has two stages: *samatha* and *vipassana*. (HighLab found *samatha* level meditation offered a more fulfilling buzz than *vipassana* and so we include it here.) Dhammakāya followers believe *samatha* level meditation can make the mind peaceful and stable, allowing one to overcome the Five Hindrances—sensual desire, anger, sloth, restlessness, doubt. Doing so enables them to enter a state of mind, which they refer to as "one-pointedness," that is free from any thought.

Get High Now

There are three methods to attaining one-pointedness at the *samatha* level. HighLab found the following hybrid Samatha Level Dhammakāya Meditation to be effective:

Sit comfortably on the floor or in a chair. Breathe in deeply through your nose to a count of five; exhale to a count of five. Do this about five times. Relax. *Slowly* concentrate your mind around your nostrils as you breathe. Focus there a moment. Now concentrate on the inside corner of your right eye for a few breaths. Keep breathing. Switch your focus every few breathes to the top of your head, top of your mouth, middle of your throat, then your stomach. After you've made this round focus all your breath to the point two fingers above your belly button. Inhale, exhale in this point about ten times.

Now imagine a crystal ball within the center of your body, in your lower chest. Spend a few moments concentrating on this. Focus on the crystal ball becoming larger within you, slowly filling up your body. Relax. If you'd like, softly say the mantra "samma-araham." While still focusing on the crystal ball, feeling it centered within you, repeat the mantra with each slow exhale. Do this thirty times. A feeling of balance and tranquility will fill your body and stay with you the rest of the day.

DREAM RECORDS

No, we're not talking about the witchy, Stevie Nicks–penned slow-dance anthem on Fleetwood Mac's 30-million-selling epic song-cycle *Rumors*, which, allegedly was recorded over a sleepless month in the studio while the entire band underwent an epic binge of Bolivian Marching Powder. What we *are* talking about is an excellent method to induce audio hallucinations in states of sleep.

You know when you see a train or a truck or a ship in a dream and you hear them toot a loud horn? It sounds real. You wake shortly after and realize this dream horn was actually your alarm clock going off. Dream Records manipulate this phenomenon by manually installing prescribed noises via external repetition to induce a hypnopompic illusion . . . *um, sorry, the academic-language-bullshit meter just shorted out there. Our technicians are on it. Let's try it again* . . . Dream Records are sounds played while you are sleeping. These sounds enter your dreams and create odd and interesting dream experiences.

Get High Now

You'll need two people for this high. One assumes the Dreamer role, the other assumes the Player.

Step One: Dreamer chooses a song with which she wants to experiment. (HighLab recommends "On My Own" by Patti LaBelle & Michael McDonald, and "Next" by Scott Walker.) Place a boombox or stereo speaker on a nearby bedstand. Dreamer falls asleep as she usually would (lots of exercise earlier in the day and Dill, page 95, help). Player stays awake, waiting until Dreamer is asleep for at least ten minutes. Player can test if Dreamer is asleep by lightly waving a hand in front of Dreamer's face and seeing if she reacts—this method worked for HighLab.

Step Two: Once Dreamer is asleep, Player starts the song at a very low volume. Player should hold this volume for about five minutes, or until the song is finished—whichever comes first—then repeat or continue the song, slowly and subtly increasing the volume. The point is to let the song absorb into the Dreamer's dream for as long as possible without waking Dreamer. Continue this process, repeating the track until Dreamer finally wakes. Dreamer then recounts if and how the song entered and affected her dreams. These recollections can be fantastically weird and at times oddly poignant.

HighLab: Getting Results

Two members of HighLab who participated in the Dreamer role of Dream Records experiments shared strikingly similar experiences. While in their second night's sessions of Dream Records, both recognized the song the Player was playing and used it as a cue to enter a lucid dream. Then, when the Dreamers listened to the songs in waking hours, they recalled vivid details of the previous night's dreams they had previously forgotten. Both members likened the experience to a kind of dream flashback. They loved it. You might, too. Grab a friend and give it a go tonight.

PSEUDO-TOMATIS HEALING SOUNDS ⑤

If we cannot hear a certain frequency in our ears, we will not be able to vocalize that frequency in our throats. This is what Dr. Alfred Tomatis (1920–2001) learned studying opera singers. Though their vocal capabilities were fine, some singers were having trouble hitting notes that had previously been easy. They wanted to know why.

Tomatis discovered that after prolonged exposure to high volumes, the middle ears of the singers had become flabby, a kind of "callus" had developed to protect the eardrum from extended exposure to loud noises. (Opera nerds: Please fill in your own *Maria Callas* pun here.) As a result the singers lost the ability to sing the notes blocked by this "flab" in their ears. To cure the ailment, Tomatis developed a sound therapy in which music switched on and off in fast repetition. He theorized the therapy would "exercise" the flabby part of the middle ear back into shape, allowing the singers to hear the frequencies again, and thus sing them. It worked. Tomatis soon after became one of the most influential sound therapists of the twentieth century.

Tomatis' next goal was to improve the learning abilities of those with autism and pervasive development disorder (PDD). He knew our ears were connected to opposite parts of the brain: The right ear was connected to the left brain, the left ear was connected to the right brain. The left brain is where we process language. Tomatis argued that those who hear most sounds through their right ears—*right ear dominant*—can learn and interpret language quickly and accurately because their ears are directly wired to the language-areas of the left brain. Those who are *left ear dominant* will process information more slowly and less reliably because the sound is sent to the right brain, which can't process it, and is thus re-sent across the corpus callosum to the left brain. The additional time it takes the left ear to send information from the right brain across the corpus callosum to the left brain affects language processing ability, generates errors, and causes learning disorders.

> **Fun Fact:** *Consider the sounds "b" and "p," two letters we can only distinguish through their higher harmonics. People who are left ear dominant have to guess the difference between these letters, which delays their response and leads to errors. Those with right ear dominance understand the distinction between the letters instantly.*

To retrain left ear dominant people to hear with an "ideal listening curve," Tomatis developed gated and filtered audio tracks, a sound therapy of high frequencies that stimulates the brain. He claimed gating and filtering could help lessen the symptoms of dyslexia, attention deficit disorder, autism, and depression, as well as boost creativity and performance. Numerous studies over the last twenty years show Tomatis therapy did indeed increase language comprehension and processing by up to 90 percent. A study of 400 children in Toronto found that after Tomatis therapy children showed 86 percent improvement in attention span, 89 percent improvement in communication abilities, and more. A dozen more studies show similar results. (However, a 2007 study conducted at University of California, Berkeley, countered these claims.)

Even people without learning disorders can benefit from Tomatis sound therapy. By stimulating the brain through gating and filtering, Tomatis argued, "normal" people could improve motor skills, improve overall sound processing, and gain physical energy (i.e., get high). For his groundbreaking contributions, Tomatis was named Knight of Public Health in 1951.

Get High Now

Many of Tomatis sound therapy products are available online, and, as always, we urge the curious to explore further. Meanwhile, *just for you*, we enlisted the HighLab Audio Department to create a sound clip on Gethighnow.com that helps give the sense of the gating and filtering audio technique of Tomatis sound therapy.

Listen to the Psuedo-Tomatis Healing Sounds for at least ten minutes prior to a mentally challenging task and you'll see, hear, and feel a difference. More importantly, it creates a clear-headed, sparkling aural buzz.

Funner Fact: *Different languages use different frequencies: Britons speak English in frequencies between 2,000 and 12,000 Hz; the French speak their language in frequencies mainly between 1,000 and 2,000 Hz. Tomatis theorized that the discrepancy in pitches between these languages makes the French "deaf" to English and vice versa. He believed this is the primary reason it is so difficult for Britons and French to learn one another's language.*

SATANIC BINOCULAR VISION

The word binocular is a compound of the Latin *bini* (double) and *oculus* (for the eye). Having two eyes gives humans a wider field of vision, up to 200 degrees, as well as depth perception. Binocular vision also enables utrocular discrimination, allelotropia, fusion, and . . . OK, yeah, you're thinking: That's fine and all, but can having two eyes get me high? Yes, Chaka, we're happy to say it can. Here's how.

Get High Now

Hold this book in one hand at arm's length level with your eyes. Focus on Satan. Now with your free hand touch your thumb to the end of your nose, while continuing to focus on Satan. Move your thumb out from your nose while continuing to keep your focus on Satan. Holy Jesus! The devil hath framed two thumbs around thy Satan! Now switch your focus to your thumb. My Sweet Satan, there are now two Satans framing your thumb! O Devil, you are a wicked one!

TRANSPERSONAL BANDING

A formless energy level containing the platonic sense of primordial light and the primordial sound representing a level between the "no" self and energetic ground, and . . . you know, trying to summarize in simple terms some of these 1970s meditation highs is like trying to translate a book written in Esperanto without knowing Esperanto . . . and without having access to an Esperanto dictionary. That's because most of the authors of these

1970s meditation books had no idea what they were talking about. They were high. And so soon you shall be, after trudging through the below descriptor paragraph. Hurry, we're almost there . . .

OK, deep breath. *Transpersonal* is a term used to describe the category of psychology related to stages of consciousness that go beyond rational but precede mystical. *Banding*: We have no idea what that means. The people who practice this exercise refer to it as the "upper four levels of new humanistic ventures." Together, from what we were able to understand, the title Transpersonal Banding refers to getting in contact with intrinsic levels of thinking and acting, of "banding" to your primordial self. By doing this we can become aware of our qualities of compassion, generosity, humor, strength, and courage, and thus are more open to the energy of matters of the heart and mind. Phew. Enough of that—it's high time.

Fun Fact: *One of the most influential British writers of the twentieth century, Aldous Huxley was also a famous mystic and an early adopter of parapsychology. Huxley could lull himself at will into a state of deep meditation, then transport his mind anywhere he wanted to go—usually to fantastical places. Once there, he would report smells, tastes, feelings, and other vibrant sensations. Huxley's was not a dream state; he would never go unconscious, but would rather shift part of his consciousness into an imaginary world while leaving his faculties of speech in a totally conscious state. Doing this allowed him to clearly and consciously communicate his subconscious visions. How did he do it? Nobody knows, but his assistants believe rigorous practice in self-hypnosis and powerful self-suggestion played a large part.*

Get High Now

It is best to attempt Transpersonal Banding after Sudarshan Kriya or Twelve-Cycle Meth Breath (pages 63; 158).

Step One: Sit in a chair. Relax your arms to your side. Take a few breaths in through your nose, to the count of about *four*. Relax. Imagine yourself falling down to earth, through the soil, traveling deeper. Now imagine falling down to nearly the center of the earth, deeper still. Once you are at the center, stop and rest within the soil. Look around, feel around.

Step Two: Now, find a rock, a gem, the first thing that catches your eye. Look at it. Watch as it grows brighter, as it shines up, getting bigger. The light begins to fill the earth. It enters your body, there, sitting in the chair. You feel it enter your right heel then slowly move up your feet through your leg. Keep breathing slow, deep breaths through your nose.

Step Three: You now feel the light making its way to your right hand, elbow, and up to the top of your neck. The light moves to your left side, starting at the shoulder and working down, finally exiting back to earth from your left heel, creating a circuit through you. Breathe. Stay there, feel the energy transbanding for a few minutes. Go on for as long as you'd like. When you are finished, you will feel lighter on your feet and a comforting warmth in your body and mind.

SUPRABHATAM

While retiring in a Punjab restaurant one night from a grueling 12-hour high session—after which every HighLab member swore off ever trying to get ripped again—we were unwittingly taken on an auditory hallucination, one more powerful than any we had experienced in the previous month, so altogether pure and fulfilling we were reapprised of the sheer power and virtue of *getting high*.

It was a song, more, a chant, a group of children singing unrhymed lyrics in perfect synchronization to a marshal beat, each word swirling into the next, each phrase punctuated with a cadence that seemed tied to the rhythm of our beating hearts. There was something primal and frightening about it, yet soulful and otherworldly. Above all, it was comforting and beautiful.

The server told us it was from the Indian music/chant style called *Suprabhatam*, a traditional Sanskrit hymn that is chanted in the morning to awaken Hindu gods. Since their inception in sixteenth-century India, Suprabhatam have become a part of the daily ritual for millions of Hindus worldwide. Our server woke to Suprabhatam every morning in his village, the voices from the school nearby echoing against the mud walls of his room. To remind him of home, he played Suprabhatam in the restaurant. We eat there often.

Get High Now

A number of DJs and producers have taken Suprabhatams and made slick, danceable tracks from them. Shiva should smack these clowns with his many palms.

What you want are older, traditional Suprabhatams. Children singers are a *big plus*—they add a mystical, almost eerie quality to this already cosmic chanting. We've had luck with Gopika Poorni-ma's *Gayatri Mantras*, which were taken from traditional mantras repeated three times in the day—morning, noon, and evening—up to 108 times as a means for Hindus to attain God.

SALAMANDER (Do Not Do It)

This slimy amphibian has been used to cure various ailments for over two thousand years, first with the Greeks in the first century A.D. and later for Europeans. The great seventeenth-century alchemist John Hartman claimed that rubbing pulverized salamander on your gums would help to extract rotten teeth. Hartman's ground-breaking research, rediscovered by author Richard Rudley, has unfortunately not yet been embraced by the American Dental Association, but modern scientists have found, shockingly, that he was not too far off. Lab tests show salamander secretions contain the alkaloid *samandarin*, a neurotoxin similar to local anesthetics.

Truth be told, of all the amazing reptilian highs in this book (Toads, page 160), salamander is the one least proven to work. But before you start complaining about why we're featuring it here, consider that the medicinal myth of the 'mander is long established. There must be *some* reason Hartman and the Greeks spent so much time writing about it, and now there's at least a little scientific data (samandarin = local anesthetic) to suggest the ancients might have been right.

The sad fact is in the last fifty years scientists have been spending too much time curing cancer (boring!) than dazzling their minds and numbing their gums with salamander neurotoxins. This is one of the few reptilian hallucinogenic growth industries yet to be exploited. Get to work!

Get High Now

. . . but be careful. As well as promoting their significant medicinal and magical qualities, ancient alchemists also warned that salamanders were deadly poisonous. If taken in large enough doses, the alkaloid samandarin can cause death. Do Not Eat Salamanders To Get High.

PINWHEEL ◉

Known as Messier 101, the Pinwheel is a spiral-shaped galaxy about 170,000 light-years in length located 27 million light-years away from earth. It was discovered by Pierre Méchain in 1781, a gifted astronomer who had to abandon his passion for stargazing and turn to hydrography and coastline surveying to support himself. His discovery of the Pinwheel was later featured in the Messier Catalog, where it got its commonly used scientific name.

You wanted to learn about the Pinwheel *Galaxy*, right? What? No? You just want to get *high* instead? Typical. Ok, see below.

Get High Now

Stare at it for five minutes. Then look at a large white area—a wall, paper, desk. A hodgepodge of negative and positive afterimages and distorted perspective awaits.

SHEPARD-RISSET GLISSANDO ⦿

If you're anything like HighLab, you too were totally amazed by the Shepard Tones (page 38). For this reason, we're going to hang out a bit with Shepard's cohort, the famed French electric music composer Jean-Claude Risset, and have ourselves more mind-boggling good times listening to this related audio high, the Shepard-Risset Glissando. Come join us, won't you?

What you'll be hearing is the constantly descending note-by-note configuration of the Shepard Tones woven into a continuous, fluid signal. The audio loops over and over but sounds as if it were continuously getting lower and lower in pitch—like a balloon slowly deflating but never becoming flat.

Get High Now

Click on the Shepard-Risset Glissando link at Gethighnow.com. Headphones help but aren't necessary. Start the track.

Though HighLab found this audio high to be not as effective as the original Shepard Tones, it still completely spaced us out . . . for, like, hours. It helps to imagine the tone as constantly descending. Just tell yourself it keeps going down, then listen, then go . . . down.

DREAMLIGHT MASKS

Lucid dreaming (page 99) is a dream in which you realize you are dreaming. For some people, like us, it can be one of the strangest, most fun highs attainable.

In 1993, Stephen LaBerge, Ph.D., developed the NovaDreamer, a mask designed to extend and deepen lucid dreams. It works by monitoring the eyes for back-and-forth motion, which occurs in REM sleep. Sensors in the NovaDreamer identify this movement then begin pulsing electric lights that filter through the closed eyelids. While dreaming, the wearer recognizes these lights as coming from the NovaDreamer mask and the dream becomes lucid. A HighLab member who has used NovaDreamers claims it to be a totally otherworldly, indescribably odd experience.

Get High Now

Production of NovaDreamers stopped in 2006 while a new, advanced model is in development. As of winter 2009, Nova-Dreamers are hard to find and expensive, ranging from about $200 to $300. Alternatively, numerous sites offer do-it-yourself dream-light masks for the electronically inclined. Though expensive to buy, and kind of a pain to make, most owners claim NovaDreamers are worth the money and effort, offering rich, sometimes unforgettable subconscious experiences.

PARTNERED BREEMA

Part massage, part meditation, Breema is a yoga-like practice designed to relax the body and mind while creating a "balanced state of energy." It was discovered somewhat mysteriously in Breemava, "a mountain village in the Near East" by chiropractor Jon Schreiber in 1980. The techniques are done either as a pair or solo, with the goal of making participants feel nurtured rather than drained by their bodies. Breemans tout that the practice improves immunity, organ function, circulation, and more.

HighLab found Breema to be an effective way of feeling relaxed and a bit "floaty" for a few hours. One HighLab participant found it a great way to get his girlfriend interested in having sex with him. We do what we must.

To get a "proper" Breema treatment, go to a certified instructor. Following are doggerel examples of two partnered exercises HighLab found pretty groovy.

Get High Now

Assign a Breemer One (relaxer) and Breemer Two (practitioner).

Leg Bend:

Step One: While laying on the ground, Breemer One places his feet on the torso of Breemer Two, just above the hipbones. Breemer Two then slowly leans over Breemer One's body, bending his knees so that they fold onto his lower chest. Hold for a count of ten.

Step Two: Breemer Two then softly cups Breemer One's ankles, placing her finger under his leg around the Achilles heel, and slowly extends the legs out. The full extension should take about five seconds. Repeat this leg bend about three times or as long as is comfortable. And remember, neither Breemer should feel any strain nor pressure during any part of the exercise.

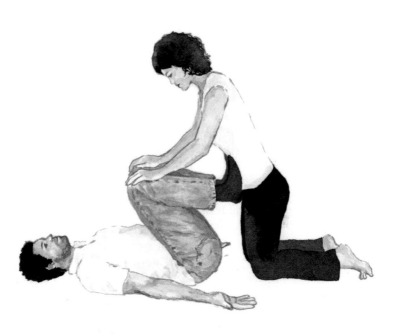

Back Rock:

Step One: Breemer One lies belly down on the floor. He is to stay in this position, fully relaxed, for the entire exercise. Breemer Two approaches, kneels down, and holds Breemer One by the shoulders, rocking his body side-to-side, focusing on gently moving his spine just off the floor with each rock. Breemer Two does this for about a minute.

Step Two: Next, Breemer Two moves her hands around beneath the arms and down to the small of Breemer One's back, continuing the gentle rocking back and forth. Between rocks, Breemer Two lightly brushes Breemer One's back with the tips of her fingers. The entire exercise should last about five minutes, but can go on as long as both partners would like.

When done, switch roles. By the end of a round, both Breemers will feel a soft tingliness, a feeling of balance and clarity . . . or at a minimum, according to one HighLab member, "kinda turned on, actually."

> **Fun Fact:** *The nine principles of harmony in Breema exercises read like song titles from an early-1980s soft soul record. They are: body comfort; firmness and gentleness; mutual support; no haste/no pause; no force; individual movement/individual activity; non-judgmental environment; full participation; no more extras. Can't you just hear the reverbed snare, fretless bass, and soft pitter-patter of congas? We can, or maybe that's just the gauzy Breema high we're on as we write this.*

CLARY SAGE BATH ☺

A biennial herb, clary sage is known by its strong odor, described by one HighLab associate as "a walk in the woods with a touch of Thanksgiving." Some (us) find it very grandma-ish and are turned off by the smell; others find it sexy. Either way, it's not the odor of clary sage that gets us high; it's the phytochemicals. These naturally occurring chemical compounds have been used as pain relievers for millennia. Among phytochemicals is salicin, a chemical extracted from bark of the willow tree, from which aspirin was synthetically modeled.

Clary sage was called *Oculus Christi* in the Middle Ages, which translates to the "Eye of Christ," because it was a popular antiseptic for cleaning mucus in the eye. It was also used as a folk remedy for infertility. Today, clary sage is used primarily in baths, in which it acts as a very strong, very stony sedative.

HighLab is apprehensive when it comes to aromatherapies (we prefer hallucinating in a bath of Schizophrenic Blood, page 75). However, our trusty HighLab associate, Jennifer, swore the clary sage bath produced one of the finest highs she has ever tried— and she's tried *many*. We, too, were convinced after her impassioned description: "[When I'm in a clary sage bath] it feels like a party is going on inside of me; it's a small, intimate get-together where they play smooth R&B and drink Hennessey. And when I emerge I feel as soft as a baby's bottom. Actually that's wrong— I feel as soft as *my* bottom . . . after it's been soaking in a warm tub with clary sage."

Get High Now

Fill a bath and drop in about six drops of clary sage extract. About ten minutes later be prepared for the soul train to drop you off in Highsville. Choo-choo!

⚠ WARNING: Mixing alcohol with clary sage has a very intense narcotic effect. Bathers should avoid booze while in the clary sage bath.

CIRCULAR BREATHING

Ever wonder how Kenny G can hold such beautifully long notes on his shiny saxophone? Or how that oboist can toot the haunting phrase at the beginning of *The Rite of Spring* in the upper register for what seems like minutes? It's not the three shots of whiskey these gentlemen slammed before taking the stage: It's *circular breathing.*

By storing air in the cheeks, expelling that air into the instrument, blocking the throat and simultaneously breathing in through the nose (if it sounds like there is a lot going on here, it's because there is) a player can exhale continuously while nourishing his body with fresh air.

In 1998, Geovanny Escalante of Costa Rica used circular breathing to set the world record for holding a single note: 1 hour, 30 minutes, and 45 seconds. Consider, if you don't play a wind instrument, how cool it would be to go to a baseball game, sit behind the umpire, and blow a dog whistle nonstop for the *entire* nine innings. At the end of the game, you could stand up and yell at the ref: "Strike Four, bitch: *You're* out!"

Get High Now

Step One: Take a breath in through your nose, inhaling deeply. As you exhale, balloon your cheeks with air. Keep your cheeks full as you continue to breathe in and out through your nose. Do this for a few breaths until you feel comfortable.

Step Two: Inhale again through your nose but this time make a small passage in the middle of your lips. Slowly relax your ballooned cheeks by gently blowing air out of that passage. Place a finger at your lips; you should be able to feel air coming out. (While doing this make sure air is only coming from your cheeks; do not push air out of your lungs.) Continue inhaling and exhaling through your nose while simultaneously loosening your cheeks to exhale air. It takes practice.

Step Three: When your cheeks are almost completely deflated, fill them back up with a burst of air from your lungs. This is known as the *switch back*. Think of your lungs and cheeks as two separate chambers: opening the chamber to let air into your cheeks, closing as you breathe from your nose into your lungs. Try *switching back* a few times. Some people can do this after a few tries; others take much longer. Stick with it.

Test It Out: Once you think you've gotten the *switch back* down and feel a steady stream of air coming from your mouth as you exhale, get a straw and a glass of water. Put one end of the straw in your mouth, the other in the water. Start circular breathing, trying to keep a continuous stream of bubbles in the water while inhaling and exhaling comfortably through your nose.

Beyond improving your brass and woodwind playing skills, circular breathing produces a nice, light-headed high—especially at the beginning stages when you are hyperventilating because you don't know what you're doing. Ah, blissful ignorance.

SYD BARRETT–DEDICATED FRACTAL ACID WORDS

Syd Barrett (1946–2006) was a founding member and vocalist/guitarist for (The) Pink Floyd, with whom he penned all the songs for the band's epic first album, *The Piper at the Gates of Dawn*. While touring for the album, Barrett would be so obliterated by LSD that he would play the same single chord on his guitar through every song of the set. Eventually, the other members of Pink Floyd kicked Barrett out of the band.

Barrett went out on his own, and while steadily losing his sanity, recorded the magnificent solo album *The Madcap Laughs*, which was followed by the mournful, disjointed, and at times graceful *Barrett*. In the early 1970s Barrett's mental facilities finally failed completely, and he moved back to his childhood home where he would spend the rest of his life living with his mother in self-imposed exile.

Get High Now

If you want to see what life might have looked like through Syd Barrett's eyes circa 1969, stare at the image below.

Note: This high works on the same perception-confusing principles of Devil's Fork (page 127) and Fraser Spiral (page 33). See those for a detailed explanation.

NYMPHAEACEAE

The family of flowering plants referred to as "water lilies," *Nymphaeaceae* are almost as common in ponds as they are on posters on dorm-room walls. It's all thanks to Claude Monet (1840–1926), the French impressionist whose most famous works feature the Nymphaeaceae—the favorite design accent for hundreds of thousands of American female freshman Art History majors over the past twenty years.

Before Nymphaeaceae were the wallpaper du jour for college students, they were a wonder drug, stocked in medicine cabinets throughout Renaissance Europe as a powerful sedative. The

Nymphaeaceae water lily shares much of the same chemical structure with apomorphine, a chemical cousin to morphine and dopamine agonist (which aids in the transmittal of dopamine). Archaeological evidence suggests that extracts from the lily were used in ancient Egypt and Mexico to induce auditory and visual hallucinations. Sadly, while Mayans and Egyptians were using Nymphaeaceae to get ripped, prudish European monks ingested the lily for its other "benefit": as a suppressant for wet dreams!

Get High Now

Nymphaeaceae is often used in shampoos for its ability to keep hair clean, shiny, manageable, and "gorgeous all day long." Some online health food sites offer Nymphaeaceae supplements claiming other benefits. HighLab cannot vouch for these suppliers as A) they have chosen the colors peach and purple for their logos; B) they have used the Dom Casual font for all copy on their sites.

But you want to get high now. In which case, do as the ancients did: Go to your neighborhood natural foods grocer, buy 5 grams of dried flowers of the White or Blue Lotus, steep them in hot water for ten minutes, strain, and drink. What you'll have is Nymphaeaceae tea, a favorite libation in many yoga and meditation circles. A HighLab associate who has tried Blue Lotus Nymphaeaceae tea reports the effects to be mild and relaxing.

⚠ WARNING: Like every other flower-based tea, the wrong quantities of the Nymphaeaceae can be toxic. Just as you wouldn't drink a gallon of chamomile tea to relax, use common sense and don't overdo it with Nymphaeaceae. Stick with 5 grams and dig the mildness.

INTERSPECIES REFLECTIVE DIALOGUE

In 1859, Charles Darwin published *On the Origin of Species*, arguing that animals evolve over time to suit their particular environments. Evolution has since become a scientific standard, no matter what some Kansans say. If we accept that animals evolve to their environments, so their brains also evolve, and so eventually will their capacity to understand language increase. If we accept all this, which, as said, most of us already do, we must also accept that animals will continue to evolve their communication skills with humans. Cats and dogs have unquestionably improved their language-response skills since their domestication about 10,000 years ago. If animals continue at the rate they have been evolving, they will eventually not only be able to take commands *from* us but give commands *to* us. Animals will some day talk. About Romanée Conti wine. About Proust. About how to get us high.

Get High Now

Talk to the animals. Help them; help us.

AWARENESS

Awareness is how we view ourselves and make sense of the world around us. It is no one thing, but a combination of processes occurring within our brains: an *internal world* of memories, perceptions, and ideas, and an *observed, external* world of visuals, audio, and tactile feelings. About half of our waking hours and 100 percent of our sleeping hours are spent in the internal world of self-reflection, in an intense dialog we share only with ourselves.

When we slip from this internal world of self-reflection into the observed, external world of vision and feelings we never realize it's happening, yet we do it thousands of times a day. To slow down and begin to bridge these two worlds, to notice the shifts from internal to outside awareness—from memory to visual stimulation, ideas to tactile feelings—is to better understand how our brains work, how we contextualize the world: why we are, where we are, and who and what we are.

Get High Now

Close your eyes. Relax. Now remember something from the recent past, like a nice night camping on the beach. Remember all the details: the sound of the crashing waves, the stars, the smell of the campfire, the breeze. Stay there for a few moments. Now bring your awareness back to the present and open your eyes. Notice how your awareness shifts from an internal world of memories, ideas, and feelings to an observed, exterior world of visual input. When you remembered back, where exactly did you go? You were physically *here*, sitting here, in the present, but most of your awareness was lost *there*, in memories, emotions, of the interior past.

How is it any less of an experience traveling to a distant land than sitting in an armchair in your house *remembering* traveling? Is it the tactile feel that is missing, that *sense* of the world? Consider that even in the present state, feeling and seeing yourself throughout the day, most of your time is spent in the interior world, perceiving and thinking through outside stimuli—you spend two-thirds of your life there, wandering and wondering in your mind alone.

The exterior world provides us with a constant flow of ingredients with which our minds form our interior world, our self-awareness, feelings, and attitudes. Some of us choose to create from these outside ingredients a view of ourselves and the world that is riddled with stress, striving, and anxiety. These people will spend their lives in disappointment. Others choose ingredients that open themselves to happiness. These people will be content and fulfilled, no matter what they do, who they are with, or where they travel—be it a trip camping on a beach or to the couch *thinking* of the beach. For them, life is wondrous.

The mind is vast; it contains multitudes. You can steer it in any direction. Choose the right path, and go. Get High Now.

ACKNOWLEDGMENTS

Without the following people this book would not have been possible. Actually, that's a lie. It would have been *totally* possible, and could well have been much better than it actually is. With that, please blame or commend these chaps and lasses as you see fit, starting with . . . Christine Boepple, Loren Chasse, Booker Lockwood, Kerry McLaughlin, Cassius Sorrel, Burt Culver, Josh Ceazan, Geoff Koops, Michael and Meredith Arthur Skryzypek, Tad Panther, and the dozens of other brave soul-searchers who checked in to HighLab from time to time (some of whom may never check out); Siri Sat "Tweets" Khalsa, M.D., for her sesquipedalian advice on all things physiological; editor-writ-large Steve "hurry-up-and-wait, wait-now-hurry-up" Mockus for thoroughly and repeatedly excoriating my arse—factually, editorially, *literally*; the patient and accented Suzanne "Brazilionairre" LaGasa for making beauteous the ugliest of written ramblings (and inviting me to all those fun brunches); Nancy Chan, whose wonderfully visceral *sumi* ink illustrations cast a soulful light into a vector world; Kelly Niland for the help early on; and last and least, Face, for keeping her cool when all those hippies were "transbanding" around her nappy bed.

HighLab Models: David Cuetter, Kim Du, William Craven, Charlotte White, Face.

ABOUT THE AUTHOR

James Nestor usually writes about architecture, alternative fuels, and popular culture for the *San Francisco Chronicle, Dwell Magazine, National Public Radio, Outside Magazine, San Francisco Magazine,* and more.

In April 2009, he covered the first-ever surfing expedition to northern Norway and Russia, in the Arctic Circle. Nestor is currently writing a book about the neuroscience of alleged out-of-body experiences. He lives in San Francisco.

QUICK SEARCH HIGH INDEX

HIGHLAB FAVORITES

MEDITATIONS

VISUAL (illustrations and exercises)